A
Treasury
of
Kate Greenaway

A treasury of

This collection © Robert Frederick Publishers

First edition 2000

4 & 5 North Parade

Bath

England

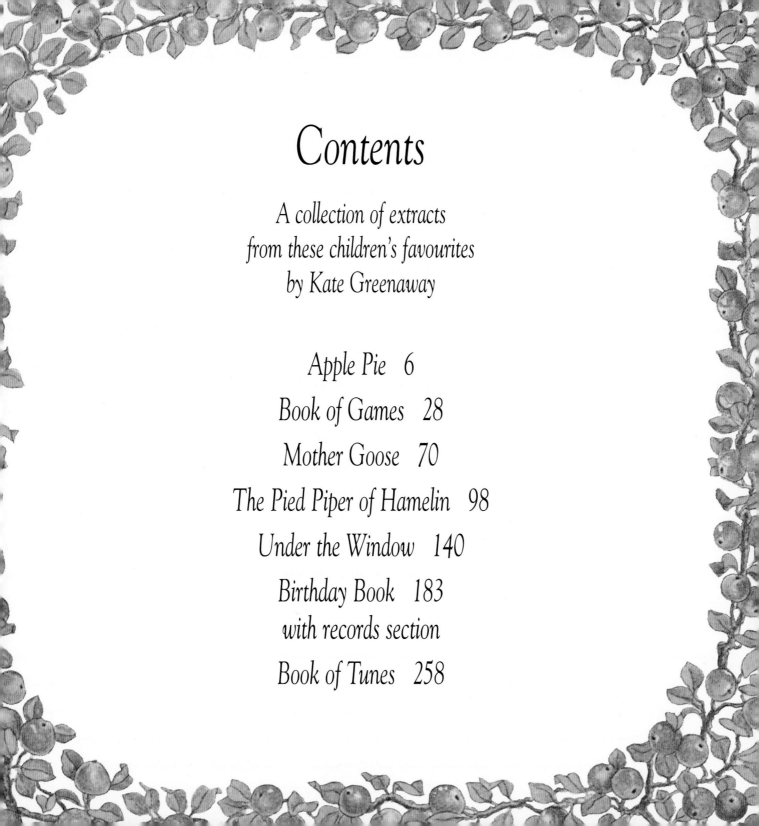

Contents

A collection of extracts
from these children's favourites
by Kate Greenaway

Apple Pie   6

Book of Games   28

Mother Goose   70

The Pied Piper of Hamelin   98

Under the Window   140

Birthday Book   183
with records section

Book of Tunes   258

A APPLE PIE

By
KATE GREENAWAY

APPLE PIE

A APPLE PIE

APPLE PIE

B BIT IT

APPLE PIE

C

CUT IT

APPLE PIE

D DEALT IT

APPLE PIE

E EAT IT

APPLE PIE

F FOUGHT FOR IT

APPLE PIE

G

GOT IT

H HAD IT

J JUMPED for IT

APPLE PIE

K
KNELT FOR IT

L
LONGED FOR IT

M MOURNED for IT

APPLE PIE

N NODDED FOR IT

APPLE PIE

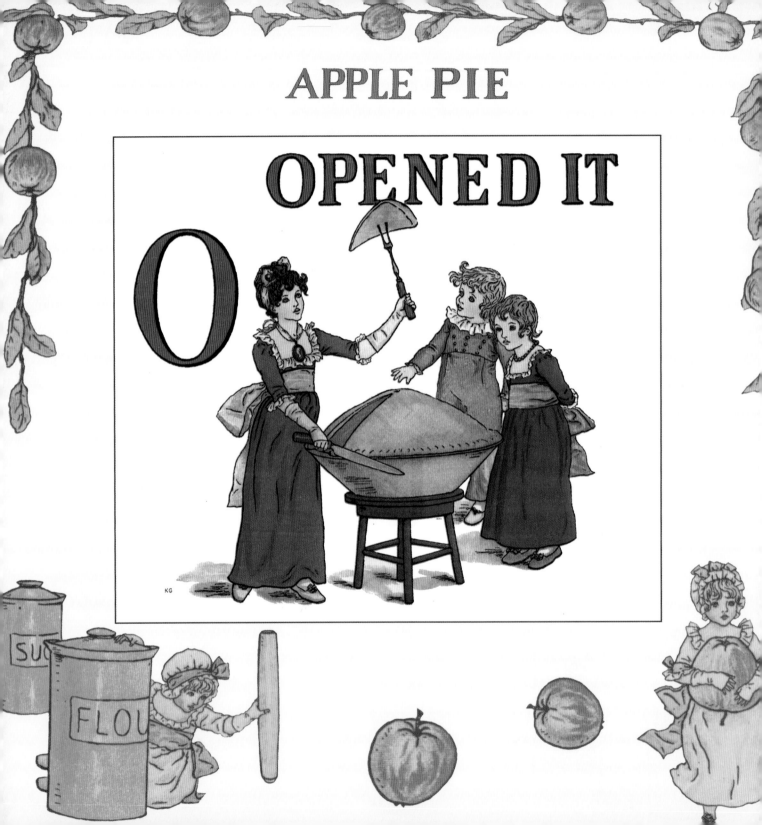

OPENED IT

O

APPLE PIE

P PEEPED IN IT

APPLE PIE

Q QUARTERED IT

R

RAN FOR IT

K.G

FLOU

APPLE PIE

S

SANG FOR IT

APPLE PIE

T TOOK IT

APPLE PIE

UVWXYZ

ALL HAD A LARGE SLICE
AND WENT OFF TO
BED

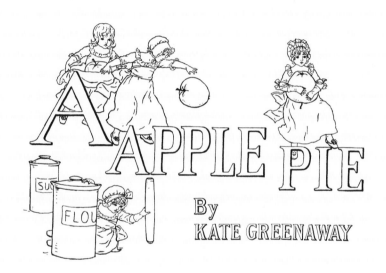

A APPLE PIE

By
KATE GREENAWAY

Book of Games

Selections from the original,
written & illustrated by Kate Greenaway

SKIPPING

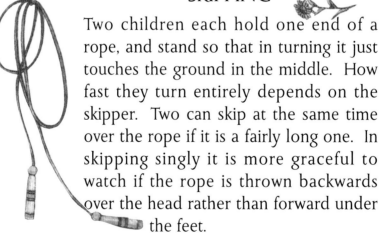

Two children each hold one end of a rope, and stand so that in turning it just touches the ground in the middle. How fast they turn entirely depends on the skipper. Two can skip at the same time over the rope if it is a fairly long one. In skipping singly it is more graceful to watch if the rope is thrown backwards over the head rather than forward under the feet.

PUSS IN THE CORNER

The child who represents puss stands in the middle, while the others stand at fixed stations round her. One then beckons to another saying: "Puss, puss, give me a drop of water!" when each runs and changes places. Puss then runs and tries to get into one of the places, if she succeeds, the one left out is puss.

TOPS

Tops are common enough objects to most people, but there is some skill required in spinning them. There are also many different games. For "Peg in the Ring" (played with a peg top), draw a circle about three feet in diameter. One player begins by throwing his top into the centre, and whilst it is spinning the other players peg their tops at it, but if it gets out of the ring, and ceases spinning, the owner may pick it up and peg it at any others spinning in the circle. To set whipping tops going, they should be rapidly twirled round with the hands, and whipped, not too hardly at first. An eel skin makes the best kind of whip. Races can be played with whip tops, the boy who can whip his top along at the greatest speed is the winner. Another game called "Encounters" consists in the players whipping their tops against each other till one of them falls.

TEAPOT

One player leaves the room, while the others decide on a word with many meanings. The absent player having been called in, his object is to find out the chosen word. To enable him to do this, the others converse about it, but instead of using the word itself, say "tea-pot" instead. For instance, if the word chosen be "rain," the players converse about it in the following manner: "We shall have 'tea-pot' (rain) tonight. When I was riding yesterday, the 'tea-pot' (rein) broke. The 'tea-pot' (reign) of Queen Victoria has been long and glorious." When the player correctly guesses the hidden word, the person whose remark enabled him to do so, leaves the room in his turn.

TWENTY QUESTIONS

One of the players is sent out of the room, and the others agree upon some subject, which he is to discover by asking twenty questions; and they must all be of such a nature as can be answered by "Yes" or "No."

WHAT IS MY THOUGHT LIKE?

One player thinks of some person or object and then asks each of the others in turn: "What is my thought like?" Each names some object and the leader then announces what his thought was; and each player is requested to prove the resemblance between his guess and the subject really chosen. If he cannot he must pay a forfeit.

HUNT THE RING

A ring is threaded on a long piece of string with the ends joined. The players stand in a circle, the cord passing through their closed hands. The ring circulates from one to another, while a player in the centre of the circle endeavours to find it. When he does so, the person in whose hand the ring is found takes his place.

SEE-SAW

A great deal of amusement may be derived from having a see-saw. It should be made of a thick plank of wood balanced over a fallen tree-trunk or other suitable erection. The players sit on the ends, balancing themselves as equally as possible, and go up and down. If one player will stand in the middle to work it, he can help to balance it and prevent a sudden jerk should anyone fall or get off without warning.

MARBLES

Many and various are the games which can be played with marbles. "Ring-taw" is a very favourite pastime. Two cir-  cles are drawn on the ground, the outer one six feet in diameter, the inner one nine inches. The players put one or more marbles inside the inner circle, and shoot one at a time from the outer ring at them. As long as a player does not send a marble out of the ring he may shoot indefinitely. When they have all fired once, they shoot from the place where their marbles remained, not the original starting place. If a player drives a marble out of the circle he wins it and shoots again, but if his "taw" remains in he is out, and must put a marble in the circle. There are other games called "Conqueror," "Increase Pound," "Three Holes," "Lag Out," and "Snops and Spans."

UP JENKINS

The company divide into two parties and sit round a table. One party then puts their hands under the table and a shilling or other small article is placed in one of the palms. The other side then calls out "Up Jenkins!" and the players whose side has the shilling concealed must all place their closed hands on the table. The opposite side must then guess in which hand the shilling is concealed. The hands that they think have not got it must be told to go down, but if one of those hands should contain it, the player must show it, and the same side hides the shilling again. But if all the hands but one are sent down without the shilling being found, then the player must give it up, and the opposite side hides it in the same manner.

TOUCH WOOD

All the children but one place themselves in various positions, each touching something that is wood. They keep constantly running from one wooden thing to another. The one left out runs after them, and the first she catches not touching wood takes her place.

BATTLEDORE & SHUTTLECOCK

This is a most convenient game, because one solitary individual can find amusement as well as any number, provided there is a bat for each player. The object of the game is to keep the shuttlecock going as long as possible.

HUNT THE SLIPPER

The children sit on the ground, or on low seats in a circle, with their knees raised. One has been left out; she brings a slipper, and giving it to one child says:

"Cobbler, cobbler, mend my shoe,
Get it done by half-past two."

She goes away, and comes back in about a minute and asks if it is done. (During this time the slipper has been passing round.) The child answers, she thinks her neighbour has it; so the seeker passes on to her, and getting the same answer she has to go round till the slipper is found. If she is a long time finding it, the slipper may be thrown across the circle.

EARTH, AIR, FIRE & WATER

The players form a circle, and one stands in the centre holding a handkerchief knotted into a ball. He counts up to ten, then throws the ball into someone's lap, calling out either "Earth", "Air", "Fire", or "Water". If he cries "Earth", the person in whose lap the handkerchief has fallen must instantly name some animal which lives on the earth; if the word was "Water", some fish must be named; if "Fire", something that can exist in fire; if "Air", some bird. If he allows the ball-thrower to count up to ten without his answering he must pay a forfeit.

THE FEATHER GAME

The players sit close together, and one of them taking a piece of swansdown (or similar substance), blows it up into the air. The other players must keep it afloat by their breath; if anyone allows it to sink to the ground he must pay a forfeit.

MULBERRY BUSH

The children form into a ring, and holding hands
run round and sing:

"Here we go round the mulberry bush,
The mulberry bush, the mulberry bush;
Here we go round the mulberry bush
On a cold and frosty morning."

Then unloosening hands they pretend to wash them, and say:

> "This is the way we wash our hands,
> Wash our hands, wash our hands;
> This is the way we wash our hands
> On a cold and frosty morning."

They then go round in a ring again and sing "mulberry bush," to be again followed by pretending to wash faces, dresses, go to school, and anything they like.

THE STORY GAME

One of the players starts an original story, and leaves off in a very exciting place; his left-hand neighbour must instantly continue it, and also stops at an exciting place, when the thread of the story is resumed by the player on his left hand. For example, one player starts the following story: "One evening, several centuries ago, a knight was riding through a dark wood, when, hearing a noise, he looked up and saw—" Here the player stops, and his left-hand neighbour continues: "A band of robbers rapidly advancing towards him. He gave himself up for lost, when—" The story is continued by left-hand neighbour, and so the game goes on till the tale is finished by the last player.

TOM TIDDLER'S GROUND

One part of the field or lawn is marked off as Tom Tiddler's ground, over which Tom presides in solitary state. It is supposed to have a quantity of lumps of gold scattered about it. The other players venture on, and pre-

tend to be picking up something, at the same time singing; "Here I am on Tom Tiddler's ground, picking up gold and silver!" He rushes after them, and if he succeeds in catching anybody, that one has to take his place as Tom Tiddler. Tom may not leave his own ground.

FOX & HEN

One of the players is chosen to be fox and another to be hen. All the others are chickens, and form a string at the back of the hen one behind another. They then advance to the fox's den and ask him the time. They repeat the question several times till he says it is twelve o'clock at night, when they must instantly run away as the fox will pursue them, the hen dodging the fox and trying to prevent his seizing the last chicken. When all the chickens have been captured the game is finished.

PROVERBS

One of the party is sent out of the room while the others choose a proverb. When one is selected each person in turn takes a word of the proverb which he must bring into his answer when questioned by the absent player, who asks a question of each in turn, and from their answers guesses the proverb.

HOP SCOTCH

Chalk out on the ground a figure like the accompanying diagram. Then the players "pink;" that is, throw their piece of tile, or lead, towards the pudding, or top of the figure. The one who lodges his tile there begins; if more than one succeeds in doing this, they "pink" again. The winner begins by standing at *, and throwing his tile onto the division marked 1; he then hops into the space and kicks the tile out to the starting point. Then he throws the tile into 2; hops into 1, then into 2, and kicks the tile out as before. He repeats this through the different numbers till he arrives at 8; here he may put his feet into 6 and 7 and rest himself, but he must begin hopping again before he kicks the tile home. He then goes on through 9, 10, 11, as before directed. 12 is another resting-place, where he may put down both feet. When he comes to plum pudding he must kick the tile with such force that it goes through all the other beds by one kick. In the other divisions it is not necessary to kick the tile so hard, as the player may hop as many times as he likes. If he throws the tile into a wrong number, or if it rests on a line, he loses his innings, whether kicking it out or throwing it in to begin with. He also misses his turn if he puts his feet down in what is not a resting-place, or if he puts his feet on a line, or kicks the tile outside the diagram.

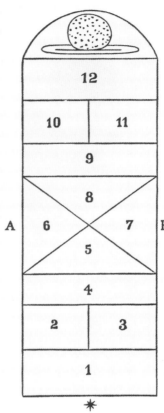

THE HAT GAME

A hat is placed on the ground, and the players (standing two or three paces from it) try to throw cards, one at a time, into it. This sounds much more easy to do than it really is.

ORANGES AND LEMONS

The two tallest players, taking the name of orange and lemon respectively, join hands, and holding them up form an arch under which the others pass in single file, holding on to each others' dresses, singing:

"Oranges and lemons," say the bells of St.. Clements.
"Brickbats and tiles," say the bells of St.. Giles.

"You owe me five farthings," say the bells of St. Martin's.
"When will you pay me?" say the bells of Old Bailey.
"When I grow rich," say the bells of Shoreditch.
"When will that be?" say the bells of Stepney.
"I do not know," says the great bell of Bow.
Here comes a candle to light you to bed,
And here comes a chopper to chop off your head!

When the last one comes below the arms they descend and catch him, and he is asked in a whisper if he will be orange or lemon. He whispers the answer and joins whichever he has chosen holding on round her waist. The game continues thus till all are caught, when a tug-of-war ensues between the parties.

MUSICAL CHAIRS

Someone plays the piano. Chairs must be placed down the room, back to back, one less in number than the players who galop round them in time to the music. Suddenly it stops, and everybody then tries to get a chair, but as there is one short, someone will be left standing, and is then out of the game. A chair is taken away and the game goes on as before till only one player, the victor, is left.

HOOPS

Every child knows, or ought to know, the pleasure of bowling a hoop. What a nice ring there is about it, when on a fine frosty day the juvenile members of the family all turn out with hoops and race along the road. There is a very jolly game called "turnpikes," but it wants rather an open space; any number can play, only half the players need hoops. Two largish stones or bricks are placed side by side about six inches apart at regular intervals in a circle or along a road, each pair being guarded by a "pike-keeper." The bowlers, who all stand in a row, start at some little distance off and drive their hoops between the bricks. If they succeed in doing this, they steer round and go through again; but should anyone miss, he takes the place of the "pike-keeper" whose gate he missed and the "pike-keeper" becomes a bowler.

MAGIC MUSIC

The company sit in a circle, and one person is sent out of the room. Then the players either hide or alter something in the room or agree that the absent one shall do something, such as repeat a verse of poetry, etc. When they have decided the player is called in, and may ask whether it is something to find, alter, or do. He is told which it is, and someone must then begin playing on the piano. When he is near finding, altering or doing the thing decreed, the music is loud; but when he moves away from the thing hidden or altered, or does not guess what he has to do, the music is soft. It is by listening to its sound that the player is guided in performing his task.

HIDE-AND-SEEK

One child called "he" must hide his eyes at a place called "home", while the other children run and hide. When they are hidden they call whoop! Then "he," uncovering his eyes, runs out and tries to catch them before they can get "home." The one caught is "he" next time. If none are caught, then the same one must be "he" again.

SWINGS

A swing is the source of much innocent enjoyment which most children can have for a very small outlay. It consists of two upright posts, with a bar securely fastened horizontally; to this two ropes are tied to which a seat is attached. A bough of a tree is a more picturesque place for a swing, but trees are not always to be had for the wishing. Boat swings at fairs are irresistible attractions to most boys.

FROG IN THE MIDDLE

The child who represents the frog sits on a hassock in the
middle of the room, all the other children
run and dance round, singing:

"Frog in the middle, you can't catch me!
Frog in the middle, you can't catch me!"

"Frog" must try to catch them with her hands without getting up from her stool; the one who is caught has to take the place of "Frog."

RUSSIAN SCANDAL

The players sit in a circle and the leader whispers some anecdote or quotation to his left-hand neighbour, which he in turn repeats to the person next to him, and so the story is whispered round the circle, the last player relating aloud what has been told him. The original is then repeated, and it is amusing to see how entirely different the two narratives are.

THE ADJECTIVE GAME

One of the players leaves the room, while the others agree on an adjective which the absent player has to discover by questioning the others in turn. They must answer the questions in such a manner as will illustrate the adjective they have chosen. For instance, if they have fixed upon "abruptly," each player must answer the question put to him in an abrupt manner.

BLIND MAN'S BUFF

One child has her eyes blindfolded with a handkerchief so that she cannot see and is placed in the middle of the room. The children say to her: "How many horses has your father got?" She replies: "Three!" Children: "What colours are they?" She: "Black, White and Grey!"

Children: "Turn round three times and catch who you may!" They then turn her round three times, and she tries to catch anyone she can; the one caught has to be the next "blind man."

THE SHEPHERDESS AND THE WOLF

The players stand in a row at one end of the lawn while the shepherdess stands at the other. Half-way between the wolf must be concealed behind a bush. The shepherdess then calls out: "Sheep, sheep, come home!" One of the sheep replies: "I'm afraid of the wolf!" The shepherdess then says: "The wolf has gone to Devonshire and won't be home for seven years; sheep, sheep, come home!" The sheep then singly try to reach the shepherdess without being caught by the wolf. And so the game continues till all the players have either been caught by the wolf or reached the shepherdess safely.

THE HIDDEN WORD

One of the players leaves the room, while the others agree on a word. The absent player is then called in, and asks questions in turn of the others, who must all bring into their answers the word previously agreed upon. By this means the hidden word is guessed.

SOAP BUBBLES

Make a lather of soap and warm water, into which dip
a clay pipe; blow through it, a bubble
then issues from out the bowl — a
wonderful transparent globe, glorious with iridescent colours.

FOLLOW-MY-LEADER

An active and daring boy should be chosen as leader, the others follow him one behind the other, as closely as they can, doing as he does, and going where he goes, over gates, stiles and obstacles of all kinds. If anyone fails in accomplishing any one feat, he takes his place behind the rest. The next one who fails goes behind him, and so the game continues until the leader chooses to stop.

KITES

Most boys and girls know how to make and fly a kite. On a fine windy day, what can be more delightful than a good run over a common or breezy hill. Even a wet day need not come amiss; it gives a good opportunity for mending them or for making new ones. Japanese kites made in the shape of birds are amusing novelties and look very imposing. Paper "messengers" of all descriptions may be sent up the string; as they speed up, turning rapidly round and round, they can be followed by the eye till they reach the kite. Parachutes are also easily made, but as no string is attached, they are not so readily captured again.

TIRZA, OR DOUBLE TAGG

The players stand in pairs one behind another in the form of a circle facing the centre. There must be two odd players, one of whom runs away while the other catches. Directly the player who is being pursued places himself in front of any couple he is safe, while the hindermost person of the trio becomes the pursued. If he is caught before placing himself in front of another couple, he becomes the pursuer.

PROHIBITIONS

The players decide to dress a lady, but the following colours — green, yellow, blue and pink must not be used. One player asks of each in turn: "How will you dress my lady?" One says: "In a white silk dress!" Another: "With a wreath on her head!" and so on. Whoever mentions the forbidden colours pays a forfeit.

DOLLS

Most little girls like to possess a large family of dolls, though they may vary more in size and shape than an ancient Egyptian and a nineteenth century Master. There are the tiny little dolls which lie in

uncomfortable attitudes in dolls' houses decked out in bright colours. There is the Dutch doll, with it stiffly-jointed legs and arms. There is the heavy old-fashioned wooden doll, as large as a good-sized baby. And now we have dolls which open and shut their eyes and say "Papa!" "Mamma!" Anyone who wishes to become a good needlewoman should try making dolls' clothes, where neat work is essential to the look of the thing.

BUZ

This is a very old game. All the players sit in a circle and begin to count in turn, but when the number 7, or any multiple of 7 cones, they say "buz" instead. If anyone forgets this, he is put out and the game commences over again. "Fiz" for five makes a variety.

SHADOW BUFF

A small sheet or table cloth must be fastened up at one end of the room. "Buff" sits facing it. A light is placed on a table a short distance behind "Buff," all the others in the room being extinguished. The players then pass in succession between "Buff" and the light, distorting their features and performing various odd antics, in order to make their shadows entirely different to their ordinary appearance. "Buff" must then guess whose shadow it is, when he guesses correctly, that player takes his place.

BALL

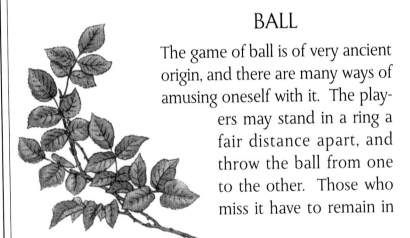

The game of ball is of very ancient origin, and there are many ways of amusing oneself with it. The players may stand in a ring a fair distance apart, and throw the ball from one to the other. Those who miss it have to remain in the attitude in which they were when they dropped the ball. At the end of the game the circle presents a very grotesque appearance. Another way is that whoever misses goes out of the game, so that the circle diminishes till only two remain; these continue till one fails and leaves the other the winner. A more exciting way is for the players to take the names of the days of the week, or, if more than seven, the months of the year. Then, for instance, Monday says; "The ball falls to Thursday." Thursday catches it and says; "The ball falls to Tuesday," and so on. Whoever misses pays a forfeit. Throwing the ball to the ground and letting it bounce before catching it, or making it bounce against a wall are other varieties of the game.

RUTH & JACOB

One person is blindfolded, and the rest dance in a circle round him till he points at some one. That person enters the ring, and the blind man calls out "Ruth"; "she" answers "Jacob"; and moving about within the circle so as to elude the blind man, continues to answer "Jacob" as often as the blind man calls out "Ruth." This continues until "Ruth" is caught. "Jacob" must then guess who it is he has caught; if he guesses correctly, "Ruth" takes his place, and the game goes on as before; if wrongly, the same one is "Jacob" again.

MARY'S GONE A-MILKING

All the children stand in a row, with joined hands,
       except one, who stands in front of them,
       and is Mother. They advance and retreat,
       singing:
          "Mary's gone a-milking,
              a-milking, a-milking;
        Mary's gone a-milking,
           dearest mother of mine!"

To which the Mother replies (advancing and retreating):

> "Take your pails and go after her, after her, after her;
> Take your pails and go after her, dearest daughters of mine!"

Children: "Buy me a new pair of milking pails,
milking pails, milking pails;
Buy me a new pair of milking pails,
dearest mother of mine!"

Mother: "What's your father to sleep in, sleep in, sleep in;
What's your father to sleep in, dearest daughters of mine?"

Children: "Sleep in the washing-tub," &c
Mother: "What am I to wash in?," &c
Children: "Wash in a teacup," &c
Mother: "A teacup won't hold your father's shirt," &c
Children: "Wash in a thimble," &c
Mother: "A thimble won't hold the baby's cap," &c
Children: "Wash in the river," &c
Mother: "Suppose the clothes should float away," &c
Children: "Take a boat and go after them," &c
Mother: "Suppose the boat was to sink with me," &c
Children: "Then there'd be an end of you!" &c

Mother here rushes after the children. If she succeeds in catching one,
that one must be Mother.

QUEEN ANNE AND HER MAIDS

One child covers her eyes, while the others, standing in a row close to each other, put their hands behind them. One has a ball concealed, which all pretend to have. They then call the one who has covered her eyes, and addressing her sing:

> "Queen Anne, Queen Anne, she sits in the sun;
>   As fair as a lily, as brown as a bun;
>   She sends you three letters, and begs you'll read one!"

To which Queen Anne replies:
>   "I cannot read one unless I read all,
>   So please Miss Mabel* deliver the ball."

If she has guessed correctly, the one who had the ball takes Queen Anne's place; but if it was a wrong one she hides her eyes again while the ball changes hands.

* Or whatever the name of the one she thinks has it is.

GENERAL POST

One person is selected as "postman" and blindfolded, the others all take the names of different places, except one, who is chosen as leader, and has a written list of the places chosen by the players. He then calls out: "The post is going from London to York," or any other names as the case may be. The persons named must then exchange seats, the "postman" trying to catch them as they move. Sometimes "general post" is called out, when all change their seats. Whoever is left out becomes "postman."

Mother Goose

or the

Old Nursery Rhymes

Illustrated by Kate Greenaway

HARK! hark! the dogs bark,
The beggars are coming to town;
Some in rags and some in tags,
And some in silken gowns.
Some gave them white bread,
And some gave them brown,
And some gave them a good horse-whip,
And sent them out of the town.

Johnny shall have a new bonnet,
And Johnny shall go to the fair;
And Johnny shall have a blue ribbon,
To tie up his bonny brown hair.

We're all jolly boys, and we're coming with a noise,
Our stockings shall be made
Of the finest silk,
And our tails shall trail the ground.

Elsie Marley has grown so fine,
   She won't get up to serve the swine;
   But lies in bed till eight or nine.
   And surely she does take her time.

Daffy-down-dilly
    has come up to town,
In a yellow petticoat
    and a green gown.

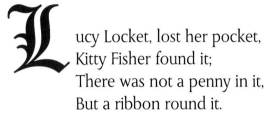

Lucy Locket, lost her pocket,
Kitty Fisher found it;
There was not a penny in it,
But a ribbon round it.

There was a little boy and a little girl
Lived in an alley;
Says the little boy to the little girl,
"Shall I, oh, shall I?"
Says the little girl to the little boy,
"What shall we do?"
Says the little boy to the little girl,
"I will kiss you!"

Jack and Jill
Went up the hill,
To fetch a pail of water;
Jack fell down
And broke his crown,
And Jill came tumbling after.

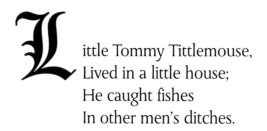

Little Tommy Tittlemouse,
Lived in a little house;
He caught fishes
In other men's ditches.

𝕿ell Tale Tit,
Your tongue shall be slit;
And all the dogs in the town
Shall have a little bit.

Mary, Mary, quite contrary,
How does your garden grow?
With silver bells, and cockle shells,
And cowslips all of a row.

Goosey, goosey, gander,
Where shall I wander?
Up stairs, down stairs,
And in my lady's chamber;
There I met an old man,
Who would not say his prayers;
Take him by the left leg,
Throw him down the stairs.

A dillar, a dollar,
A ten o'clock scholar;
What makes you come so soon?
You used to come at ten o'clock,
But now you come at noon!

L ittle Betty Blue,
Lost her holiday shoe.
What will poor Betty do?
Why, give her another,
To match the other,
And then she will walk in two.

illy boy blue, come blow me your horn,
The sheep's in the meadow, the cow's in the corn;
Is that the way you mind your sheep,
Under the haycock fast asleep!

Girls and boys come out to play,
The moon it shines as bright as day;
Leave your supper, and leave your sleep,
And come to your playmates in the street;
Come with a whoop, come with a call,
Come with a good will, or come not at all;
Up the ladder and down the wall,
A halfpenny loaf will serve us all.

ere am I, little jumping Joan,
When nobody's with me,
I'm always alone.

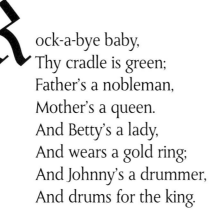

Rock-a-bye baby,
Thy cradle is green;
Father's a nobleman,
Mother's a queen.
And Betty's a lady,
And wears a gold ring;
And Johnny's a drummer,
And drums for the king.

Little Tom Tucker,
He sang for his supper.
What did he sing for?
Why, white bread and butter.
How can I cut it without a knife?
How can I marry without a wife?

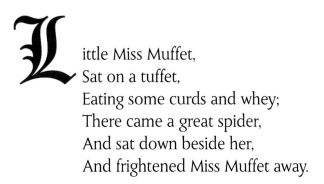

L ittle Miss Muffet,
Sat on a tuffet,
Eating some curds and whey;
There came a great spider,
And sat down beside her,
And frightened Miss Muffet away.

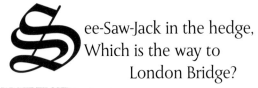

See-Saw-Jack in the hedge,
Which is the way to
London Bridge?

Little lad, little lad,
Where wast thou born?
Far off in Lancashire,
Under a thorn;
Where they sup sour milk
From a ram's horn.

My mother, and your mother,
Went over the way;
Said my mother, to your mother,
"It's chop-a-nose day."

ne foot up, the other foot down,
That's the way to London town.

eorgie Peorgie, pudding and pie,
Kissed the girls and made them cry;
When the girls begin to play,
Georgie Peorgie runs away.

As Tommy Snooks, and Bessie Brooks
Were walking out one Sunday;
Says Tommy Snooks to Bessie Brooks,
"To-morrow—will be Monday."

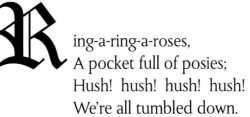Ring-a-ring-a-roses,
A pocket full of posies;
Hush! hush! hush! hush!
We're all tumbled down.

The Pied Piper
of Hamelin

by Robert Browning

Illustrated by Kate Greenaway

I.

amelin Town's in Brunswick,
By famous Hanover city;
The river Weser, deep and wide,
Washes its wall on the southern side;
A pleasanter spot you never spied;
But, when begins my ditty,
Almost five hundred years ago,
To see the townsfolk suffer so
From vermin, was a pity.

II.

ats!
They fought the dogs and killed the cats,
And bit the babies in the cradles,

And ate the cheeses out of the vats.

And licked the soup from the cook's own ladles,

Split open the kegs of salted sprats,

Made nests inside men's Sunday hats,

And even spoiled the women's chats,

By drowning their speaking
With shrieking and squeaking

In fifty different sharps and flats.

III.

At last the people in a body
To the Town Hall came flocking:

"Tis clear," cried they, "our Mayor's a noddy;
"And as for our Corporation—shocking
"To think we buy gowns lined with ermine
"For dolts that can't or won't determine
"What's best to rid us of our vermin!
"You hope, because you're old and obese,
"To find in the furry civic robe ease?
"Rouse up, sirs! Give your brains a racking
"To find the remedy we're lacking,
"Or, sure as fate, we'll send you packing!"

At this the Mayor and Corporation
Quaked with a mighty consternation.

IV.

An hour they sate in council,
At length the Mayor broke silence:
"For a guilder I'd my ermine gown sell;
"I wish I were a mile hence!
"It's easy to bid one rack one's brain—
"I'm sure my poor head aches again.
"I've scratched it so, and all in vain
"Oh for a trap, a trap, a trap!"
Just as he said this, what should hap
At the chamber door but a gentle tap?
"Bless us," cried the Mayor, "what's that?"
(With the Corporation as he sat,
Looking little though wondrous fat;
Nor brighter was his eye, nor moister
Than a too-long-opened oyster,
Save when at noon his paunch grew mutinous
For a plate of turtle green and glutinous)
"Only a scraping of shoes on the mat?
"Anything like the sound of a rat
"Makes my heart go pit-a-pat!"

V.

"Come in!"—the Mayor cried, looking bigger:
And in did come the strangest figure!
His queer long coat from heel to head
Was half of yellow and half of red,

And he himself was tall and thin,
With sharp blue eyes, each like a pin,
And light loose hair, yet swarthy skin
No tuft on cheek nor beard on chin,
But lips where smile went out and in;
There was no guessing his kith and kin:
And nobody could enough admire
The tall man and his quaint attire.
Quoth one: "It's as my great-grandsire,
"Starting up at the Trump of Doom's tone,
"Had walked this way from his painted tombstone!"

VI.

He advanced to the council-table:
And, "Please your honours," said he, "I'm able,
"By means of a secret charm, to draw
"All creatures living beneath the sun,
"That creep or swim or fly or run,
"After me so as you never saw!
"And I chiefly use my charm
"On creatures that do people harm,
"The mole and toad and newt and viper;
"And people call me the Pied Piper."

(And here they noticed round his neck
A scarf of red and yellow stripe,
To match with his coat of the self-same cheque;
And at the scarf's end hung a pipe;
And his fingers they noticed were ever straying
As if impatient to be playing
Upon his pipe, as low it dangled
Over his vesture so old-fangled.)
"Yet," said he, "poor Piper as I am,
"In Tartary I freed the Cham,
"Last June, from his huge swarms of gnats,
"I eased in Asia the Nizam
"Of a monstrous brood of vampyre-bats:
"And as for what your brain bewilders,
"If I can rid your town of rats
"Will you give me a thousand guilders?"
"One? fifty thousand!"—was the exclamation
Of the astonished Mayor and Corporation.

VII.

Into the street the Piper stept,
Smiling first a little smile,
As if he knew what magic slept
In his quiet pipe the while;
Then, like a musical adept,
To blow the pipe his lips he wrinkled,
And green and blue his sharp eyes twinkled,
Like a candle-flame where salt is sprinkled;
And ere three shrill notes the pipe uttered,
You heard as if an army muttered;

And the muttering grew to a grumbling;
And the grumbling grew to a mighty rumbling;
And out of the houses the rats came tumbling.
Great rats, small rats, lean rats, brawny rats,

Brown rats, black rats, grey rats, tawny rats,
Grave old plodders, gay young friskers,
Fathers, mothers, uncles, cousins,
Cocking tails and pricking whiskers,
Families by tens and dozens,
Brothers, sisters, husbands, wives—
Followed the Piper for their lives.

From street to street he piped advancing,
And step for step they followed dancing,

Until they came to the river Weser
Wherein all plunged and perished!
—Save one who, stout as Julius Caesar,
Swam across and lived to carry
(As he, the manuscript he cherished)
To Rat-land home his commentary:
Which was,

"At the first shrill notes of the pipe,
"I heard a sound as of scraping tripe,
"And putting apples, wondrous ripe,
"Into a cider-press's gripe:
"And a moving away of pickle-tub-boards,
"And a leaving ajar of conserve-cupboards,
"And a drawing the corks of train-oil-flasks,
"And a breaking the hoops of butter-casks:
"And it seemed as if a voice
"(Sweeter far than by harp or by psaltery
"Is breathed) called out, 'Oh rats, rejoice!
" 'The world is grown to one vast drysaltery!
" 'So munch on, crunch on, take your nuncheon,
" 'Breakfast, supper, dinner, luncheon!'
"And just as a bulky sugar-puncheon,
"All ready staved, like a great sun shone
"Glorious scarce an inch before me,
"Just as methought it said, 'Come, bore me!'
"—I found the Weser rolling o'er me."

VIII.

Y ou should have heard the Hamelin people
Ringing the bells till they rocked the steeple

"Go," cried the Mayor,
          "and get long poles,
"Poke out the nests
          and block up the holes!
"Consult with carpenters
          and builders,
"And leave in our town not even a trace
"Of the rats!" —

when suddenly up the face
Of the Piper perked in the market-place,
With a,

          "First, if you please,
          my thousand guilders!"

IX.

A thousand guilders! The Mayor looked blue;
So did the Corporation too.
For council dinners made rare havoc
With Claret, Moselle, Vin-de-Grave, Hock;
And half the money would replenish
Their cellar's biggest butt with Rhenish.
To pay this sum to a wandering fellow
With a gipsy coat of red and yellow!
"Beside," quoth the Mayor with a knowing wink,
"Our business was done at the river's brink;
"We saw with our eyes the vermin sink,
"And what's dead can't come to life, I think.
"So, friend, we're not the folks to shrink
"From the duty of giving you something to drink,
"And a matter of money to put in your poke;
"But as for the guilders, what we spoke
"Of them, as you very well know, was in joke.
"Beside, our losses have made us thrifty.
"A thousand guilders! Come, take fifty!"

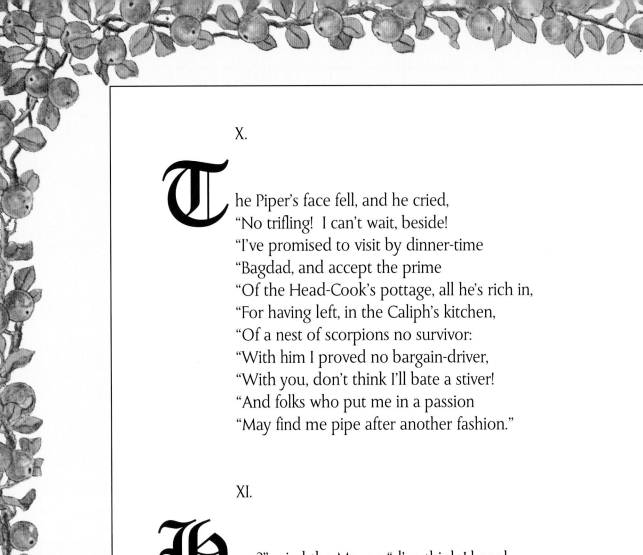

X.

The Piper's face fell, and he cried,
"No trifling! I can't wait, beside!
"I've promised to visit by dinner-time
"Bagdad, and accept the prime
"Of the Head-Cook's pottage, all he's rich in,
"For having left, in the Caliph's kitchen,
"Of a nest of scorpions no survivor:
"With him I proved no bargain-driver,
"With you, don't think I'll bate a stiver!
"And folks who put me in a passion
"May find me pipe after another fashion."

XI.

How?" cried the Mayor, "d'ye think I brook
"Being worse treated than a Cook?
"Insulted by a lazy ribald
"With an idle pipe and vesture piebald?
"You threaten us, fellow? Do your worst,
"Blow your pipe there till you burst!"

XII.

nce more he stept into the street,
And to his lips again
Laid his long pipe of smooth straight cane;
And ere he blew three notes

(such sweet soft notes as yet musician's cunning
Never gave the enraptured air)

There was a rustling that seemed like a bustling

Of merry crowds justling
and pitching and hustling,

Small feet were pattering,
   wooden shoes clattering,

Little hands clapping

and little tongues chattering,

Out came the children running.

All the little boys and girls,

With rosy cheeks
and flaxen curls,

And sparkling eyes

and teeth like pearls.

Tripping and skipping,

ran merrily after

The wonderful music

with shouting and laughter.

XIII.

he Mayor was dumb, and the Council stood
As if they were changed into blocks of wood,

Unable to move a step, or cry
To the children merrily skipping by.
—Could only follow with the eye
That joyous crowd at the Piper's back.
But how the Mayor was on the rack,
And the wretched Council's bosoms beat,
As the Piper turned from the High Street
To where the Weser rolled its waters
Right in the way of their sons and daughters!
However he turned from South to West,
And to Keppelberg Hill his steps addressed,
And after him the children pressed;
Great was the joy in every breast.
"He never can cross that mighty top!
He's forced to let the piping drop,
And we shall see our children stop!"
When, lo, as they reached the mountain-side,
A wondrous portal opened wide,
As if a cavern was suddenly hollowed;
And the Piper advanced and the children followed,
And when all were in to the very last,
The door in the mountain side shut fast.

Did I say, all?
    No; One was lame,

And could not dance the whole of the way;

And in after years, if you would blame
His sadness, he was used to say,—

"It's dull in our town since my playmates left!
"I can't forget that I'm bereft
"Of all the pleasant sights they see,
"Which the Piper also promised me.
"For he led us, he said, to a joyous land,
"Joining the town and just at hand,
"Where waters gushed and fruit-trees grew,
"And flowers put forth a fairer hue,
"And everything was strange and new;
"The sparrows were brighter than peacocks here,
"And their dogs outran our fallow deer,
"And honey-bees had lost their stings
"And horses were born with eagles' wings;
"And just as I became assured
"My lame foot would be speedily cured,
"The music stopped and I stood still,
"And found myself outside the hill,
"Left alone against my will,
"To go now limping as before
"And never hear of that country more!"

135

XIV.

Alas, alas for Hamelin!

There came into many a burgher's pate
A text which says that Heaven's gate
Opens to the rich at as easy rate
As the needle's eye takes a camel in!
The Mayor sent East, West, North, and South,
To offer the Piper, by word of mouth,
Wherever it was men's lot to find him,
Silver and gold to his heart's content,
If he'd only return the way he went,
And bring the children behind him.
But when they saw 'twas a lost endeavour,
And Piper and dancers were gone for ever,
They made a decree that lawyers never
Should think their records dated duly
If, after the day of the month and year,
These words did not as well appear,

"And so long after what happened here
"On the Twenty-second of July,
"Thirteen hundred and seventy-six:"

And the better in memory to fix
The place of the children's last retreat,
They called it, the Pied Piper's Street—
Where any one playing on pipe or tabor,
Was sure for the future to lose his labour.
Nor suffered they hostelry or tavern
To shock with mirth a street so solemn;

But opposite the place of the cavern
They wrote the story on a column,
And on the great church-window painted
The same, to make the world acquainted
How their children were stolen away,
And there it stands to this very day.
And I must not omit to say
That in Transylvania there's a tribe
Of alien people that ascribe
The outlandish ways and dress
On which their neighbours lay such stress,
To their fathers and mothers having risen
Out of some subterraneous prison
Into which they were trepanned
Long time ago in a mighty band
Out of Hamelin town, in Brunswick land,
But how or why, they don't understand.

XV.

o, Willy, let me and you be wipers
Of scores out with all men—especially pipers!
And, whether they pipe us free from rats or from mice,
If we've promised them aught, let us keep our promise!

Under the Window

Pictures & Rhymes by

Kate Greenaway

Under the window is my garden,
Where sweet, sweet flowers grow;
And in the pear-tree dwells a robin,
The dearest bird I know.

Tho' I peep out betimes in the morning,
Still the flowers are up the first;
Then I try and talk to the robin,
And perhaps he'd chat — if he durst.

Will you be my little wife,
If I ask you? Do!
I'll buy you such a Sunday frock,
A nice umbrella, too.

And you shall have a little hat,
With such a long white feather,
A pair of gloves, and sandal shoes,
The softest kind of leather.

And you shall have a tiny house,
A beehive full of bees,
A little cow, a largish cat,
And green sage cheese.

You see, merry Phillis, that dear little maid,
Has invited Belinda to tea;
Her nice little garden is shaded by trees—
What pleasanter place could there be?

There's a cake full of plums, there are strawberries too,
And the table is set on the green;
I'm fond of a carpet all daisies and grass—
Could a prettier picture be seen?

A blackbird (yes, blackbirds delight in warm weather,)
Is flitting from yonder high spray;
He sees the two little ones talking together—
No wonder the blackbird is gay!

Three tabbies took out their cats to tea,
As well-behaved tabbies as well could be:
Each sat in the chair that each preferred,
They mewed for their milk, and they sipped and purred.
Now tell me this (as these cats you've seen them)—
How many lives had these cats between them?

Little Fanny wears a hat
Like her ancient Grannie;
Tommy's hoop was
(think of that!)
Given him by Fanny.

M argery Brown, on the top of the hill,
Why are you standing, idle still?"
"Oh, I'm looking over to London town;
Shall I see the horsemen if I go down?"

"Margery Brown, on the top of the hill,
Why are you standing, listening still?"
"Oh, I hear the bells of London ring,
And I hear the men and the maidens sing."

"Margery Brown, on the top of the hill,
Why are you standing, waiting still?"
"Oh, a knight is there, but I can't go down,
For the bells ring strangely in London town."

L ittle wind, blow on the hill-top,
Little wind, blow down the plain;
Little wind, blow up the sunshine,
Little wind, blow off the rain.

Indeed it is true, it is perfectly true;
Believe me, indeed, I am playing no tricks;
An old man and his dog
    bide up there in the moon,
And he's as cross as
    a bundle of sticks.

School is over,
Oh, what fun!
Lessons finished,
Play begun.
Who'll run fastest,
You or I?
Who'll laugh loudest?
Let us try.

ittle Polly, will you go a-walking today?"
"Indeed, little Susan, I will if I may."
"Little Polly, your mother has said you may go;
She was nice to say 'Yes;' she should never say 'No.' "

"A rook has a nest on the top of the tree—
A big ship is coming from over the sea:
Now, which would be nicest, the ship or the nest?"
"Why, that would be nicest that Polly likes best."

As I was walking up the street,
The steeple bells were ringing;
As I sat down at Mary's feet,
The sweet, sweet birds
were singing.

As I walked far into the world,
I met a little fairy;
She plucked this flower,
and, as it's sweet,
I've brought it home for Mary.

152

Five little sisters walking in a row;
Now, isn't that the best way for little girls to go?
Each had a round hat, each had a muff,
And each had a new pelisse of soft green stuff.

Five little marigolds standing in a row;
Now, isn't that the best way for marigolds to grow?
Each with a green stalk, and all the five had got
A bright yellow flower, and a new red pot.

In go-cart so tiny
 My sister I drew;
  And I've promised to draw her
   The wide world through.

We have not yet started—
 I own it with sorrow—
  Because our trip's always
   Put off till to-morrow.

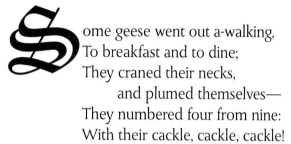

Some geese went out a-walking,
To breakfast and to dine;
They craned their necks,
            and plumed themselves—
They numbered four from nine:
With their cackle, cackle, cackle!
They thought themselves so fine.

A dame went walking by herself,
A very ancient crone;
She said, "I wish that all you geese
Were starved to skin and bone!
Do stop that cackle, cackle, now,
And leave me here alone."

You are going out to tea to-day,
So mind how you behave;
Let all accounts I have of you
Be pleasant ones, I crave.

Don't spill your tea, or gnaw your bread,
And don't tease one another;
And Tommy mustn't talk too much,
Or quarrel with his brother.

Say "If you please," and "Thank you, Nurse;"
Come home at eight o'clock;
And, Fanny, pray be careful that
You do not tear your frock.

Now, mind your manners, children five,
Attend to what I say;
And then, perhaps, I'll let you go
Again another day.

Poor Dicky's dead!—
    The bell we toll,
And lay him in
    the deep, dark hole.
The sun may shine,
    the clouds may rain,
But Dick will never pipe again!
His quilt will be
    as sweet as ours—
Bright buttercups
    and cuckoo flowers.

Up you go, shuttlecocks, ever so high!
Why come you down again, shuttlecocks—why?
When you have got so far, why do you fall?
Where all are high, which is highest of all?

K.G

$\mathfrak{T}$ommy was a silly boy,
    "I can fly," he said;
      He started off, but very soon,
        He tumbled on his head.

    His little sister Prue was there,
      To see how he would do it;
        She knew that, after all his boast,
          Full dearly Tom would rue it!

iggledy, piggledy! see how they run!
Hopperty, popperty! what is the fun?
Has the sun or the moon tumbled into the sea?
What is the matter, now? Pray tell it me!

Higgledy, piggledy! how can I tell?
Hopperty, popperty! hark to the bell!
The rats and the mice even scamper away;
Who can say what may not happen to-day?

Which is the way to Somewhere Town?
Oh, up in the morning early;
Over the tiles and the chimney-pots,
That is the way, quite clearly.

And which is the door to Somewhere Town?
Oh, up in the morning early;
The round red sun is the door to go through,
That is the way, quite clearly.

The boat sails away, like a bird on the wing,
And the little boys dance on the sands in a ring.
The wind may fall, or the wind may rise—
You are foolish to go; you will stay if you're wise.
The little boys dance, and the little girls run:
If it's bad to have money, it's worse to have none.

Pipe thee high, and pipe thee low,
Let the little feet go faster;
Blow your penny trumpet—blow!
Well done, little master!

K G

olly', Peg's, and Poppety's
Mamma was kind and good;
She gave them each, one happy day,
A little scarf and hood.

A bonnet for each girl she bought,
To shield them from the sun;
They wore them in the snow and rain,
And thought it mighty fun.

But sometimes there were naughty boys,
Who called to them at play,
And made this rude remark—"My eye!
Three Grannies out to-day!"

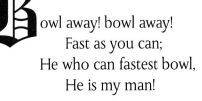

Bowl away! bowl away!
    Fast as you can;
He who can fastest bowl,
    He is my man!

Up and down, round about,—
    Don't let it fall;
Ten times, or twenty times,
    Beat, beat them all!

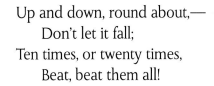

K G

or what are you longing, you three little boys?
Oh, what would you like to eat?"
"We should like some apples, or gingerbread—
Or a fine big drum to beat."

"Oh, what will you give me, you three little boys,
In exchange for these good, good things?"
"Some bread and cheese, and some radishes,
And our little brown bird that sings."

"Now, that won't do, you three little chums,
I'll have something better than that—
Two of your fingers, and two of your thumbs,
In the crown of your largest hat!"

I saw a ship that sailed the sea,
It left me as the sun went down;
The white birds flew, and followed it
To town—to London town.

Right sad were we to stand alone,
And see it pass so far away;
And yet we knew some ship would come—
Some other ship—some other day.

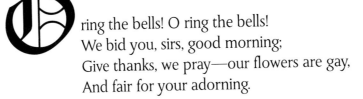

ring the bells! O ring the bells!
We bid you, sirs, good morning;
Give thanks, we pray—our flowers are gay,
And fair for your adorning.

O ring the bells! O ring the bells!
Good sirs, accept our greetings;
Where we have been, the woods are green.
So, hey! for our next meeting.

Then ring the bells! then ring the bells!
For this fair time of Maying;
  Our blooms we bring, and while we sing,
  O! hark to what we're saying.

  O ring the bells! O ring the bells!
  We'll sing a song with any;
  And may each year bring you good cheer,
  And each of us a penny.

Yes, that's the girl that struts about,
She's very proud,—so very proud!
Her bow-wow's quite as proud as she:
They both are very wrong to be
So proud,—so very proud!

See, Jane and Willy laugh at her,
They say she's very proud!
Says Jane, "My stars!— they're very silly;"
"Indeed they are," cries little Willy,
"To walk so stiff and proud."

It was Tommy
         who said,
"The sweet spring-time
         is come;
I see the birds flit,
And I hear the bees hum.

"Oho! Mister Lark,
Up aloft in the sky,
Now, which is the happiest—
Is it you, sir, or I?"

hall I sing?" says the Lark,
"Shall I bloom?" says the Fl[ower,]
"Shall I come?" says the Su[n,]
"Or shall I?" says the Show[er.]

Sing your song, pretty Bird,
Roses, bloom for an hour;
Shine on, dearest Sun,
Go away, naughty Shower!

Little baby, if I threw
This fair blossom down to you,
Would you catch it as you stand,
Holding up each tiny hand,
Looking out of those grey eyes,
Where such deep,
            deep wonder lies?

Yes, it is sad of them—
Shocking to me;
Bad—yes,
     it's bad of them—
Bad of all three.

Warnings they've had from me,
Still I repeat them—
Cold is the water—the
Fishes will eat them.

Yet they will row about,
Tho' I say "Fie!" to them;
Fathers may scold at it,
Mothers may cry to them.

ow, all of you give heed unto,
The tale I now relate,
About two girls and one small boy,
A cat and a green gate.

* * * *

Alack! since I began to speak
(And what I say is true),
It's all gone out of my poor head—
And so good-bye to you!

hat is Tommy running for,
Running for,
Running for?
What is Tommy running for,
On this fine day?

Jimmy will run after Tommy,
After Tommy,
After Tommy;
That's what Tommy's running for,
On this fine day.

A butcher's boy met a baker's boy
(It was all of a summer day);
Said the butcher's boy to the baker's boy,
"Will you please to walk my way?"

K.G.

Said the butcher's boy to the baker's boy,
"My trade's the best in town,"
"If you dare say that," said the baker's boy,
"I shall have to knock you down!"

Said the butcher's boy to the baker's boy,
"That's a wicked thing to do;
And I think, before you've knocked me down,
The cook will blow up you!"

The twelve Miss Pelicoes,
Were twelve sweet little girls;
Some wore their hair in pigtail plaits,
And some of them in curls.

The twelve Miss Pelicoes,
Had dinner every day;—
A not uncommon thing at all,
You probably will say.

The twelve Miss Pelicoes,
Went sometimes for a walk;
It also is a well-known fact
That all of them could talk.

The twelve Miss Pelicoes,
Were always most polite—
Said "If you please," and "Many thanks,"
"Good morning," and "Good night."

The twelve Miss Pelicoes,
You plainly see, were taught
To do the things they didn't like,
Which means, the things they ought.

Now, fare ye well, Miss Pelicoes,
I wish ye a good day;—
About these twelve Miss Pelicoes
I've nothing more to say.

The twelve Miss Pelicoes,
Of course, to school were sent;
Their parents wished them to excel
In each accomplishment.

The twelve Miss Pelicoes,
Played music—Fal-lal-la!
Which consequently made them all
The pride of their papa.

The twelve Miss Pelicoes,
Learnt dancing and the globes;
Which proves that they were wise, and had
That patience which was Job's.

The finest, biggest fish, you see,
Will be the trout that's
caught by me;
But if the monster will not bite,
Why, then I'll hook a little mite.

Prince Finikin and his mamma,
Sat sipping their bohea;
"Good gracious!" said his Highness, "why,
What is this girl I see?

"Most certainly it cannot be
A native of our town;"
And he turned him round to his
mamma,
Who set her teacup down.

But Dolly simply looked at them,
She did not speak a word;
"She has no voice!" said Finikin;
"It's really quite absurd."

Then Finikin's mamma observed,
"Dear Prince, it seems to me,
She looks as if she'd like to drink
A cup of my bohea."

So Finikin poured out her tea,
And gave her currant-pie;
Then Finikin said, "Dear mamma,
What a kind Prince am I!"

eigh ho!—time creeps but slow;
I've looked up the hill so long;
None come this way, the sun sinks low,
And my shadow's very long.

They said I should sail in a little boat,
Up the stream, by the great white mill;
But I've waited all day, and none come my way;
I've waited—I'm waiting still.

They said I should see a fairy town,
With houses all of gold,
And silver people, and a gold church steeple;—
But it wasn't the truth they told.

My house is red—a little house,
A happy child am I,
I laugh and play the livelong day
I hardly ever cry.

I have a tree, a green, green, tree,
To shade me from the sun;
And under it I often sit,
When all my work is done.

My basket I will take,
And trip into the town;
When next I'm there
    I'll buy some cake,
And spend my bright half crown.

Little Miss Patty and Master Paul
Have found two snails on the garden wall.
"These snails," said Paul, "how slow they walk!
A great deal slower than we can talk.
Make haste, Mr. Snail, travel quicker, I pray;
In a race with our tongues you'd be beaten to-day."

KATE GREENAWAY'S BIRTHDAY BOOK for Children

Use this section to keep the Birthday records of family and friends with notes about their special days.

Kate Greenaway's —— BIRTHDAY BOOK —— for Children

JANUARY 1ST.

WHAT are the bells about? what do they say?
Ringing so sweetly for glad New Year's Day:
Telling us all that Time never will wait,
Bidding us use it well, ere it's too late.

JANUARY 2ND.

A large brown muff, for cold, cold hands,
So dainty, too, trimmed up with bows;
Of all comforts the best, when you have
    to go out,
On a day when it freezes or blows.

JANUARY

JANUARY 3RD.

There was an old woman who shook,
The wind her umbrella it took;
   She cried, "The wind's strong,
   I can't hold it long;"
And that's why she trembled and shook.

JANUARY 4TH.

A great big muff and feathered hat,
   Poor little legs look bare;
A curious little figure this,
   Enough to make you stare.

JANUARY 5TH.

The joys of the tea-pot who will not sing?
The warmest and cosiest comforting thing!
Who does not enjoy a good cup of tea?
Without taste or reason I'm sure they must be.

6

JANUARY 6TH.

So bright, so fresh, so delightfully nice,
To skim along on the hard smooth ice!
What fun to fly on your skates away,
Skating so gaily the whole of the day!

JANUARY 7TH.

Old Mrs. Big-bonnet, little Miss Wee,
Out for an airing, as you may see;
Chatter and chatter, and pleasantly talk,
Enjoying together their nice winter's walk.

JANUARY 8TH.

Who wouldn't go to a Fancy Ball?
High-heeled shoes to make us tall;
Ribbons, and laces, and powdered head,
And then to dance a minuet led.

JANUARY

JANUARY 9TH.

I've seen many scarecrows, and Guys a few,
And I think this a frightful Guy—don't you ?
Just look at her bonnet, and look at her back !
To dress herself well she hasn't the knack.

JANUARY 10TH.

A Turk with a turban, I declare !
I think this will make you little ones stare.
Perhaps he's the Sultan, come over to see
If he in this Birthday Book will be.

JANUARY 11TH.

Dear little Baby ! he's wrapped up so warm,
 And just beginning to run :
Out in the frosty day, roses to win,
 Fresh air, and plenty of fun.

JANUARY 12TH.

A jug and a basin—for what, do you think?
With water to wash little fingers from ink ;
For some little children, alas ! are so
Fond of touching such things, you know

JANUARY 13TH.

Roly-Poly with a snowball,
Throwing it at nothing at all ;
Roly-Poly round about,
It seems to me he's very stout.

JANUARY 14TH.

So wearied with her heavy load !
 So ragged, sad, and cold !
Dear children, always pity show
 To those who're poor and old.

JANUARY

JANUARY 15TH.

A clown, or a jester, I fancy this man,
But really I can't be sure, think as I can;
His hair stands on end, and his waist's very long,
And he looks just as if he were singing a song!

JANUARY 16TH.

A cottage so rustic, and pretty, and
warm;
Would you like to live in it, pray?
Little children, I dare say, are living
there now,
And, though poor, are happy all
day.

JANUARY 17TH.

My dear little lady, now why turn your back?
I am sure that your face is fair;
Yet we see but your dress, and the round of your
cap,
Not even a vestige of hair.

JANUARY 18TH.

If you have cows, here's something
to feed them,
Something most juicy and sweet;
A fine mangold-wurzel is what cows
delight in,
To them 'tis a wonderful treat.

JANUARY 19TH.

Small black-haired child, with a chubby
round face,
Two little round eyes, and round nose;
Little fat arms, and little white frock,
And out peep the dear little toes!

JANUARY 20TH.

There was an old woman whose hat
Was all peaked, and not at all flat;
On her back was a hump,
That stuck out in a lump,—
'Twas a trouble to her when she sat.

JANUARY

JANUARY 21ST.

Of an empty chair, when it's ugly, too,
Why, what can we say, between me and you?
We only can fancy some lady fair
Is coming to sit in the empty chair.

JANUARY 22ND.

A very grand lady, come out for a walk:
    What a feather, and large-brimmed hat!
So very important, yet only a child,—
    We all very well can see that.

JANUARY 23RD.

At what a quick pace he is rushing along!
    Just look at his nose and his chin!
His hat, and his pig-tail, his curious legs,
    And his arms, too, so awkward and thin.

JANUARY 24TH.

Pray, young lady, where are you going?—
    Out for a winter's walk;
To breathe fresh air, and come home fair,
    And then some tea and talk?

JANUARY 25TH.

Useful and ornamental too,
    Handsome in colour and form
Cream-jugs may peaceful and pleasant be
    Though tea-pots sometimes have a storm.

JANUARY 26TH.

Sitting by the fireside, thinking of the past,
Of the time, long faded now, far too bright to
    last;
Waiting patiently and still, for the end to come,
Looking—with what wistful eyes!—for the last
    long home.

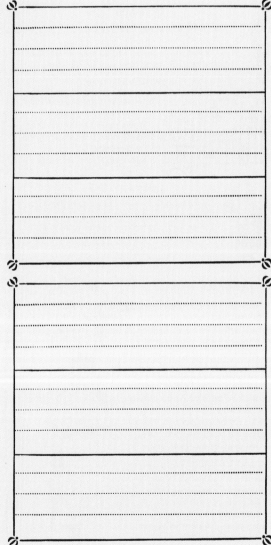

JANUARY * FEBRUARY

JANUARY 27TH.

This woman is going to market,
  With a basket full of eggs;
She has many a weary mile to walk,
  I pity her tired legs.

JANUARY 28TH.

Goosey, goosey, gander!
  With a night-cap on his head;
He turns himself, and twists himself,
  And then he goes to bed.

JANUARY 29TH.

Footstool, or hassock, whichever you call it,
  Is useful enough in its way;
But it helps little people sometimes to a tumble,
  And big people, too, I may say.

JANUARY 30TH.

What is he doing, this little Jack Horner;
  There on his three-legged stool?
Is he doing his lessons, or eating his dinner;
  Or merely just playing the fool?

JANUARY 31ST.

Baby is looking for father,
  He's been such a long time away;
Father is coming to baby,
  Has thought of her all through the day.

FEBRUARY 1ST.

Is this Queen Elizabeth, may I ask,
  With her ruff, and her cushioned head?
No, for this lady still proudly walks,
  And Queen Elizabeth's dead.

FEBRUARY

FEBRUARY 2ND.

Cabbages red, and cabbages green,
This is a fine one as ever was seen:
Cabbages grow in the garden near,
Cabbages grow the whole of the year.

FEBRUARY 3RD.

This is Master Baby, paying a morning call,
Sitting so good upon his chair, but speaking not at all;
Listening to every word, the funny little man!
Wondering at the news he hears, thinking all he can.

FEBRUARY 4TH.

Hush-a-bye, Dolly! go to your rest;
Mother wants to be busy, you know.
Dolly, be qu'et, I won't have you cry;
To sleep, child, you really must go.

FEBRUARY 5TH.

A nice new broom, to sweep away,
And keep the floor so clean;
The crumbs and dust all disappear,
There's not one to be seen.

FEBRUARY 6TH.

The wind, determined to have some fun,
Blew an old woman to make her run;
The old woman trotted along with a will,
But stopped at last, when she got to a hill.

FEBRUARY 7TH.

A kite, one day, flew up in the sky,
To try and reach the sun;
He failed, and he fell with a broken string,
And sighed, "It can't be done!"

FEBRUARY

FEBRUARY 8TH.

There was an old person too fat,
Who wore a remarkable hat;
    He said, " Let the world talk,
    I'll take a good walk,
And try to get rid of this fat '

FEBRUARY 9TH.

A shuttlecock was sent so high,
He very nearly reached the sky;
When he came down he was so vain,
They never sent him up again.

FEBRUARY 10TH.

Little maid, little maid, whither away,
Running so fast on this early-spring day?
Perhaps it's Mamma you are going to meet,
And Love lends his wings to your little feet.

FEBRUARY 11TH.

Turnips and carrots are all very fine,
If on boiled mutton you're going to
    dine;
But, as that is a dish that I really
    can't bear,
I'll willingly give up to you all my
    share.

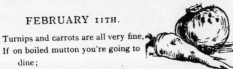

FEBRUARY 12TH.

A pot of spring flowers before me stands,
    Primroses fresh and fair;
Telling of days that are coming soon,
    When their sweetness fills the air.

FEBRUARY 13TH.

Carrying home the washing,
    Snowy-white and clean;
Merry maidens bring it home,
    As can well be seen.

FEBRUARY

FEBRUARY 14TH.

Pray, little lady, why do you come out,
When it's raining in this way?
Perhaps an important letter to post?--
I remember, it's Valentine's Day!

FEBRUARY 15TH.

Johnnie has got a new peg-top,
That spins with wonderful grace;
The boy is surprised and delighted,
Just look in his eager face.

FEBRUARY 16TH.

Polly, the milkmaid, comes over the plain,
Fills up her milk-pail, and then back again;
Milk for our breakfast, milk for our tea,
Thank the good moo-cows for you and for me.

FEBRUARY 17TH.

The old pump stands in the meadow,
Where all the cows are fed, O!
To give them a drink is but fair, I think,
So the old pump stands in the meadow.

FEBRUARY 18TH.

Little Laura Lazy lies against the wall;
If she spends her time so, she'll do no work
    at all,
Softly we will touch her, give a little shake,
Then, perhaps, this idle maid may think it
    time to wake.

FEBRUARY 19TH.

Little Tom Thumbkin blows bubbles so light,
Up they go—higher yet—colours so bright;
Little Tom Thumbkin looks quite forlorn—
His bubbles die as soon as they're born.

FEBRUARY

FEBRUARY 20TH.

An empty chair! an empty chair!
Come and sit down on it, any who dare;
It looks so firm, but give it a shake,
And into pieces it soon will break.

FEBRUARY 21ST.

"Little friend, little friend, why stare you so?"
"I'm looking, I'm looking, to see the wind blow."
"Little friend, little friend, have you a mind
To become a small pig? They alone see the wind."

FEBRUARY 22ND.

A good-sized bonnet, a very small dog,
As you can plainly see;
The bonnet would do for a kennel too,
It really seems to me.

FEBRUARY 23RD.

"Baker, what have you got in your basket?
Something good, I trust,"
"Cakes and buns, jam tarts and biscuits,
Pastry with nice thin crust."

FEBRUARY 24TH.

A Japanese tea-pot! let's have some tea,
A cup of the most delicious bohea!
Then plenty of sugar, and plenty of cream,
And with smiles of contentment our faces
will beam.

FEBRUARY 25TH.

"Dolly, Dolly, tell me, dear,
Do you like your ride?
The go-cart's small, but so are you,
There's room for more beside."

FEBRUARY * MARCH

FEBRUARY 26TH.

Do, pray, look at this lazy loon,
Smoking his pipe before it's noon!
Leaning his back against a rail,
While the little black dog is wagging his tail.

FEBRUARY 27TH.

Selina Amelia called out to her cat,—
" Oh, Pussy, dear Pussy, I wish you'd
    grow fat ;
Here's a saucer of milk, mixed with
    oil from the cod,
I hope you won't think that the mix-
    ture is odd.''

FEBRUARY 28TH.

Shall I sing to my baby about the bright flowers
  Shall I sing about the glad sun ?
Shall I sing to my baby of long summer hours ?
  Shall I sing to my sweet little one ?

FEBRUARY 29TH.

A green, green tree, that stands by itself,
  A tree without very much shade ;
For its branches are cropped quite small at top,
  Until to a point it is made.

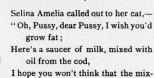

MARCH 1ST.

Not much to be seen but a feather !
Can it be on account of the weather ?
  We'll suppose a fine face,
  And a great deal of grace,
So hidden because of the weather.

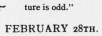

MARCH 2ND.

Upright as a dart, but without much grace,
And her grandmother's bonnet quite hides her face.
I can't say much for her—now, can you ?
And I shouldn't care to say, How do you do ?

MARCH

MARCH 3RD

Now, this I call a feat of skill,
Though I should think it made him ill,
To catch a ball, and stand like that,
Above all, when one's rather fat.

MARCH 4TH.

Miss Roundabout's dressed to go to a ball,
You'd think her so stout that she can't dance at all;
But she is so light, she's just like a balloon,
And thinks that each dance is over too soon.

MARCH 5TH.

Little Kitty, how I love you!
I like to squeeze you to my cheek;
Always purring, never scratching,
Always gentle, always meek.

MARCH 6TH.

I was walking in the country,
    It was a little sad;
This was the only creature near,
    The only friend I had.

MARCH 7TH.

Vain young person, who may you be,
Turning your head to look at me?
I will give you a penny, or give you a bun;
But compliments from me, you will have none.

MARCH 8TH.

What is she looking at, up in the sky,
    Is it the moon or the sun?
She will be dazzled, or moonstruck, perhaps,
    And then, what is to be done?

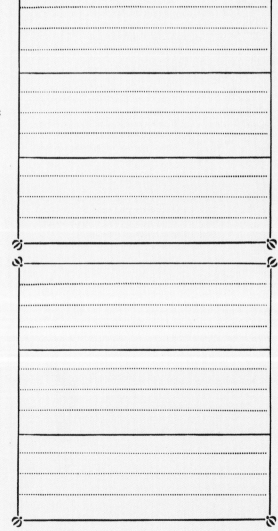

MARCH

MARCH 9TH.

Here is a round ball, give it to me,
And I will toss it up high;
Forty times as high as the house,
Then will it reach the sky?

MARCH 10TH.

Alack! alas! and well-a-day!
Here's never a child come out to play;
I'll tell Belinda, Clarissa, and Jane,
I never will promise to meet them again.

MARCH 11TH.

In this little wee house an old woman
    dwells,
She makes gingerbread figures, and
    lollipops sells;
The children all cheer her wherever she
    goes,
But she has a great trouble—which is a
    red nose.

MARCH 12TH.

"Polly, what are you looking at?
    What do you see out there?"
"I see a ship sailing far, far off;
    And where is it going?"—Ah, where?

MARCH 13TH.

A little Marionnette man,
    Throwing up a ball;
I really cannot understand
    How he can catch at all.

MARCH 14TH.

Dear little maid!—Is she sleeping,
    Or crying her woes to the ground?
Grief, and rest, and a little joy,—
    It is thus the world goes round.

MARCH

MARCH 15TH.

Baby, baby, in the bowl,
    Have you caught an eel ?
Only cotton for a line,
    To fish for Mother's reel.

MARCH 16TH.

Little Miss Sarsenet looks very glum ;
Do you think that she's cross and sulky ?—Hum !
It may be so, or it may not be ;
Miss Sarsenet's slightly ruffled, I see.

MARCH 17TH.

Sweet are the hedges close to the stile
    Laden with blossoms of May ;
Sweet sings the river that murmurs below
    The whole of the happy spring day.

MARCH 18TH.

Poor little wandering gipsy child,
    In rags, with feet all bare !
Come, bring some meat, and bread, and cake,
    And let her have a share.

MARCH 19TH.

This is the woman who is so fat,
There is no door she can get in at ;
She has a child, so very small,
That it can scarce be seen at all.

MARCH 20TH.

Strike away ! strike away !
    Make the hoop run :
The faster it rolls,
    The greater the fun.

MARCH

MARCH 21ST.

Two loving little sisters, going for a walk,
Chatter, chatter gaily, pleasantly they talk;
What do they talk of? Dolls, politics, and bees;
Both have the same views—that one plainly sees.

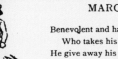

MARCH 22ND.

Benevolent and happy man,
   Who takes his walks abroad;
He give away his pence and pounds
   And all he can afford.

MARCH 23RD.

Who is coming to Margery?
Who is coming, I say?
Some dearly loved one, who brings a plum bun,—
That's who is coming, I say.

MARCH 24TH.

The wind blew hard, the wind blew strong,
And blew Lucinda fast along;
At last it blew her up in the air,
Now, has she come down, or is she still there?

MARCH 25TH.

Ah! sweet primrose, you are come,
   To tell us of the Spring;
The hedge-rows bloom, the woods are green,
   And now the birdies sing.

MARCH 26TH.

Little Patty is delighted,
   What, do you think, about
All the flowers are shooting up
   And all the buds are out.

MARCH * APRIL

MARCH 27TH.

Poor Miss Baby, in the wind,
Finds herself unsteady,
And she has to trot alone,
Until Nurse is ready.

MARCH 28TH.

Lily of the Valley, very fair to see,
Sweet and dear to all I've loved, ever dear to me.
Flower, pure and fragrant, when you begin your reign
Visions of a glad lost time will ever come again.

MARCH 29TH.

Small Billy is a coachman,
But where—oh! where's his team?
I think they're gone to Fairyland,
Or vanished in a dream.

MARCH 30TH.

The sails go round with a heavy swing,
As the wild wind plays on the hill;
And the corn is crushed, and the flour ground
Right merrily at the mill.

MARCH 31ST.

What does the child see?—is it the moon?
Or does she look at an air balloon?
Up yet higher, ever so far,
Out there peeps the evening star.

APRIL 1ST.

Look at this boy as you pass by;
Look, how he's laughing! I'll tell you why:
He made an old woman an April fool:
With vulgar boys that is the rule.

APRIL

APRIL 2ND.

A pot of flowers, if you are able,
Always have upon the table;
And a bird who'll sweetly sing:
These things tell you of the spring.

APRIL 3RD.

Baby dear, with eyes so bright,
Staring up with all your might!
What is the sight, or what the sound,
That makes your eyes so big and round

APRIL 4TH.

I am walking out so early,
    To see my great-aunt Jane;
I'll walk a mile, and talk a while,
    And then come home again.

APRIL 5TH.

Daffodils grow in the meadows,
    Scenting the April air:
Daffodils out in the garden,—
    I'm glad I have them there.

APRIL 6TH.

Running along with his flag in his hand,
    To frighten the cows away;
We see but his back, and the crown of his hat,
    His face, p'rhaps, some other day.

APRIL 7TH.

A Normandy peasant, come out for a walk:
Could you understand if you heard her talk?
"Bon jour, joli enfant," she would say,
Which means, "Pretty child, I wish you good-day."

APRIL

APRIL 8TH

Rushes by the river-side,
  Growing proud and tall;
The wind comes by, and makes them bow,
  Then they look quite small.

APRIL 9TH.

Baby, with the tea-cup,
  What have you got in it?
If it is tea, give it to me;
  Come, share it, miss, this minute.

APRIL 10TH.

Up the rope, up the rope,
  Ever so high!
Will you come down again?
  "Yes, by-and-by."

APRIL 11TH.

Birdie, dear birdie, oh, whence do you come?
  Now say, do you bring any news?
Has mother come back from London town,
  And has she not brought me new shoes?

APRIL 12TH.

What's in the basket, the basket?
  What is there, great or small?
Perhaps plum buns and gingerbread,
  Perhaps there's none at all.

APRIL 13TH.

Cowslips, cowslips, fresh and sweet,
  And very, very dear!
I look at you, and then go back—
  Oh, many a long, long year!

APRIL

APRIL 14TH.

Mermaid, or child in a sea-shell?
Pray, little mermaid, is that where you dwell?
Blown by the wind, riding over the sea,
I'd rather it you, little mermaid, than me.

APRIL 15TH.

Little hands behind you!
   And why do you hide them, then?
Have you a ball, or nothing at all
   But fat little fingers ten?

APRIL 16TH.

Would you like to know why I walk so fast?
   A sight I'm going to see;
It may be a ship, or it may be a shark.—
   It may, or it may not be.

APRIL 17TH.

Upon the grass, beneath the bright
   spring sunshine,
  There sat a gentle, pensive little maid;
The soft spring air just breathed a per-
   fume near her,
  "I bring the kisses of the flowers,"
   it said.

APRIL 18TH.

Who went in the fields to-day,
To gather marigolds, I say?
Was it Belinda Abiathar Ann?
Tell me, I pray you, if you can.

APRIL 19TH.

Dear me! this is very odd,
   Upon the stairs to sit;
I think she's got her night-gown on,
   And doesn't care a bit.

APRIL

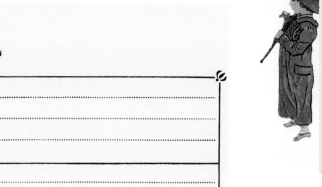

APRIL 20TH.

I want to see the world, you know;
I'm going to be a sailor:
This is my sailor suit, you see,
Just come home from the tailor.

APRIL 21ST.

Come and look at this round plate,
Hanging alone in pomp and state.
Do you like it empty, or covered with cake?
I hope it's not always like this, for your sake.

APRIL 22ND.

"Little girl, where do you come from?
    Little girl, where do you go?"
"I come from the school in the hollow,
    Where they teach us to read and to sew."

APRIL 23RD.

Yes, I am fond of them;
Now, are not you?—
Fond of potatoes,
When they are new?

APRIL 24TH.

There was an old woman whose mind
Was fixed on a race with the wind;
    Her friends said, "You'll find
    You'll be soon left behind;"
But she smiled, and set off with the wind.

APRIL 25TH.

Havė you got a cabbage there,
Little funny maiden fair?
"Yes, I have, I'm going to boil it,
Though the cook says I shall spoil it."

APRIL * MAY

APRIL 26TH.

See, O children ! now I bring
Glad sweet flowers of the spring :
May your paths with flowers be spread
May you on them lightly tread !

APRIL 27TH.

Just an entrance, nothing more ;
   Whither, whither does it go ?—
Where glad hearts are gay and light,
   Or where they ache in silent woe ?

APRIL 28TH.

Ivy, stealthily you creep,
   Killing where you cling.
Strange ! so graceful, fair a plant,
   Should be a cruel thing.

APRIL 29TH.

Blowing airy bubbles light,
Watching changing colours bright :
Tommy, happy as a king,
Joyful at so small a thing.

APRIL 30TH.

Yes, they did squabble, *scratched* in their spite;
Now they are friends again—friends again quite,
Look, how they lovingly each give a kiss;
Now we are sure that there's not much amiss.

MAY 1ST.

A strange-looking creature as ever was seen,
Dancing and grinning round Jack-in-the-green;
This is an old fashion, that comes in with May,
And sad for the sweeps if the First's a wet day.

MAY

MAY 2ND.

"Here's a nest," said a bird,
"With my eggs in it, three;
All spotted and handsome,
As eggs can well be."

MAY 3RD.

Tulips in the garden grow,
Don't they make it gay?
I'm very fond of tulips,
I'll pick one if I may.

MAY 4TH.

Little airy, fairy sprite,
Flying in the air;
Dropping blossoms to the earth,
Scattering flowerets fair.

MAY 5TH.

Is she sad, little maid,
Or is she but sleeping?
I'd rather she dozed,
Than made eyes red by weeping.

MAY 6TH.

When I was out a-walking,
I met an old, old man;
What he said, and what I said,
Now, guess it if you can.

MAY 7TH

Come, jump off the tub—just let me see
If you can do it; now—one, two, three!
Yes, you have done it; let's merrily run
Out to the fields, and we'll have fine fun.

MAY

MAY 8TH.

This girl is dressed all spick-and-span,
　　And neatly as can be ;
Her sash well tied, her mittens straight,
　　She's going out to tea.

MAY 9TH.

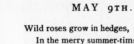

Wild roses grow in hedges,
　　In the merry summer-time,
I've talked of them, and sung of them,
　　And put them into rhyme.

MAY 10TH.

Watching how the daisies grow,
　　In the early morning ;
At night their yellow eyes are closed,
　　But open in the dawning

MAY 11TH.

"Paddy, oh Paddy, now where do you go,
Stepping an Irish jig, dancing just so?"
　　"Oh, shure I'm off, then, to Dublin town,
To buy wife and children aich a new gown."

MAY 12TH.

Blossoms pink, and blossoms white,
　　Flowering in May ;
Sweet and bright, they bloom so fair,
　　And all the world is gay.

MAY 13TH.

Such a big bonnet, a basket as big !
Is she going to market to buy a small pig?
When she comes back, it will be a fine joke,
A pig in a basket, a child in a poke.

MAY

MAY 14TH.

Up, up flies the shuttlecock, up with a jump,
Down on the battledore now, with a thump.
Fly away, shuttlecock, higher yet fly,
Up to the clouds that pass over the sky.

MAY 15TH.

A spirit floating through the night,
Where the stars now shed their light.
Tell us, tell us what you are?—
The Spirit of the Evening Star.

MAY 16TH.

Tulips in a pot, you see;
Phillis brought them in to me;
I thought Phillis very kind,
To pick her one I'd half a mind.

MAY 17TH.

Little Peggie has a dicky, and it is very tame;
She loves her bird—oh, dearly! and it loves
 her just the same;
She gives it lots of breadcrumbs, a lump of
 sugar, too:
I wish I had a bird like that, I'm sure, and so
 do you.

MAY 18TH.

Now, make haste, and go to school,
 Don't loiter here all day:
A girl should walk quite fast to school,
 And hurry on her way.

MAY 19TH.

Carry the baby over the fields,
 Carry her up the high hill;
Carry her here, and carry her there,
For baby will never be still.

MAY

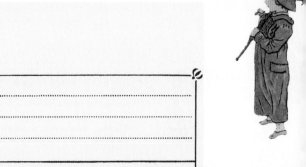

MAY 20TH.

There was an old person who feared
The sun setting light to his beard;
So he said, "I will see, and sit under a tree
Till the sun is too low to be feared."

MAY 21ST.

Do you want to hear the news?
I am dancing without shoes;
I can dance, and I can run,
I am up to any fun.

MAY 22ND.

A sweet, sweet sprig of lily-of-the-valley
Who shall have it? Little merry Sally;
She shall keep it, and wear it all day:
Lilies are found in the garden in May.

MAY 23RD.

This is Wilhelmina's back, who looks so neat and nice,
Of bread-and-butter she will take, at tea, but one
small slice;
And when she is invited to take a little more,
She always answers softly, "I had too much before."

MAY 24TH.

Out comes a fledgling, out of his shell;
He's out in the world, but he won't see it
well;
For off on his journey he's come but one
mile,
And thinks he'll go back again, to rest
awhile.

MAY 25TH.

I have a young canary,
And he loves most to dine
On fresh green dandelion leaves,
When they are young and fine.

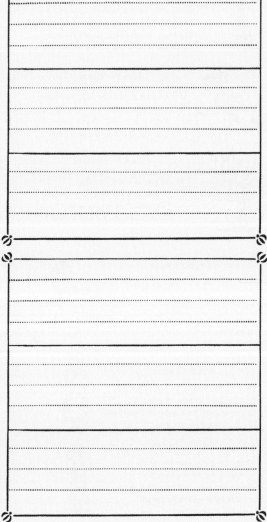

MAY

MAY 26TH.

Round you go, skipping-rope, over I fly;
Which is the happiest, think, you or I?
I am the happiest, 'tis by my will
That I skip over you, or I stand still.

MAY 27TH.

Little Bobby Balancer walks upon a rail,
If he slips and has a fall—ah! then his walks
will fail;
If he keeps his balance, and touches not the
ground,
Then Bobby'll reach his home again, lucky,
safe, and sound!

MAY 28TH.

This is Joan, she is all alone,
The others have gone to the fair;
She is rather sad, for it seems too bad
That poor Joan should not also be there.

MAY 29TH.

This is little baby's back,
Isn't it full of grace?
But you'd know how sweet she is,
If you saw her face.

MAY 30TH.

What is he doing, that fat boy,
With a bonnet on his head?
He s a lazy loon, this afternoon;
I should send him off to bed.

MAY 31ST.

Little wild flower, that grows in the field,
Ringing your merry bell!
What do you say in that tiny chime?—
Pray, little flower, tell.

JUNE

JUNE 1ST.

Windmills, like weathercocks, turn with the wind,
And change, as indeed they may;
Some little folks are exactly the same,
Perhaps this is their birthday!

JUNE 2ND.

This weak little girl sheds a tear,
She quakes and she trembles with fear;
But it's only a fish, though not in a dish,
So she need not display such great fear.

JUNE 3RD.

Warm little hearts, and wise little heads,
Gentle, and loving, and kind;
This is the way to be happy, small friends,
And that you will very soon find.

JUNE 4TH.

A rose in June, a rose in June,
That scents the summer air!
In blooming pink, I really think,
Of flowers you are most fair.

JUNE 5TH.

Baby, baby, you look like a mouse,
Holding a bonnet as big as a house.
Now, is it Granny's you've borrowed
   just now?
Do you think you may keep it?—
   will Granny allow?

JUNE 6TH.

Blossoms, blossoms on the trees
Swinging in the summer breeze,
Lending sweetness to the air,
To be shed on children fair.

JUNE

JUNE 7TH.

This is Melinda, who sits all day long,
Thoughtful and pensive, composing a song;
None wish to hear it, so people say
It is not much use her composing this lay.

JUNE 8TH.

A little girl jumped for joy,
   Upon the eighth of June;
She cried, "My birthday's come at last,
   But it will go too soon."

JUNE 9TH.

Inside the window, a lady;
   Outside, a rose-tree grows;
Kind is the beautiful lady,
   Sweet is the creeping rose.

JUNE 10TH.

I'm rather idle, as you see,
   I sit upon the ground;
And all the world seems made for me
   As it turns round and round.

JUNE 11TH.

Yes, it is sad indeed,—sad, I must say it;
That there's no croquet now, no one will
      play it.
Here stands Selina, with mallet and ball;
But no one will come and play, no one at all.

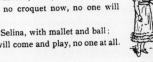

JUNE 12TH.

Ride away, ride on the branch of a tree;
How your horse canters, with action so free!
Don't ride too far, remember we're here;
Come back and tell us your travels, my dear.

JUNE

JUNE 13TH.

Gorgeous sunflower, yellow and bright,
    Turning your face to the sun;
Glorying, basking in his glad light,
    Until his day's work is done.

JUNE 14TH.

A little girl, a little girl,
    Once went to pick some flowers;
They said, "Oh, pray go home again,
    We're sure to have some showers."

JUNE 15TH.

A carnation in our garden grows;
    How pleased we are to know it!
Our gardener said we should have one,
    He said, "I'm going to sow it."

JUNE 16TH.

A pretty tree, a shady tree,
    Just casts its shadow round;
And we can go and sit beneath,
    If we don't mind the ground.

JUNE 17TH.

Janet plays at ball all day,
    Through the hot, hot weather;
Her ball is small, but very hard,
    Because it's made of leather.

JUNE 18TH.

Tiger-lily, tall and straight,
    How handsomely you grow!
Your spotted leaves, and yellow tongues—
    But stop!—you're vain, I know.

JUNE

JUNE 19TH.

Margery has a new skipping rope,
Margery skips all the day;
Bobby and Bill hate the skipping,
For Margery with them won't play.

JUNE 20TH.

Little girl leaning against the stile,
Are you resting yourself awhile?
Do you think—how sweet is the summer day,
When all the world seems made for play?

JUNE 21ST.

Little flower of the field,
To me you tell a tale,
Of blooms upon the hill-side,
Of blossoms in the vale.

JUNE 22ND.

This girl is walking to London town,
Her luncheon in her basket;
She's walking, walking up and down,
Her way—she'll have to ask it.

JUNE 23RD.

Dear moon-daisies, I love you;
Old friends, that I know so well;
Glad scenes come back when I see you,
And sad thoughts that I dare not tell.

JUNE 24TH.

Poppy, poppy, flaunting red,
In the meadow green;
You are so bold, you stare about,
And you are always seen.

JUNE

JUNE 25TH.

Against a post leant Tabitha,
    Her fan within her hand;
She looked about, did Tabitha,
    And she surveyed the land.

JUNE 26TH.

These are the two Miss Minevers,
    So good, so very good!
They each do what the other likes,
    As sisters always should.

JUNE 27TH.

I am a mountain daffodil,
    My colour it is yellow;
I think the whole world must agree
    I am a handsome fellow.

JUNE 28TH.

This is a house, it's very straight,
    And also rather tall;
And lovers of the picturesque
    Don't like this house at all.

JUNE 29TH.

This flower grows within my garden,
    Perhaps you have the same;
If that's the case, of course you know it,
    Pray therefore, tell its name.

JUNE 30TH.

There was a young person whose passion
Was always to dress in the fashion;
    That she did not succeed,
    To tell there's no need,
For you see that she's *not* in the fashion.

JULY

JULY 1ST.

There she goes with her pitchfork,
    To turn about the hay,
To toss it up, and spread it out,
    On this hot summer day.

JULY 2ND.

This is a beautiful Iris,
    Soft purple is its hue;
I think it a grand-looking flower,
    Now tell me, do not you?

JULY 3RD.

The sweetest, freshest, pinkest rose!
    The rose-tree in our garden grows,
It is sweet to sight and smell;
    Indeed, we love that rose-tree well.

JULY 4TH.

I lie beside the running stream,
And watch the clouds, and rest, and dream:
A jug with water by me stands,
Which I have filled with my own hands.

JULY 5TH.

Sitting on the wall!
It is not safe at all.
Come, come, get down, I say;
You can't sit there all day.

JULY 6TH.

How I love the field flowers,
    Blooming bright and gay!
How I love the green, green fields,
    To wander there all day!

JULY

JULY 7TH.

Most certainly I hardly know
If she has doll or baby;
Perhaps you know, you are so wise,
And think me but a gaby.

JULY 8TH.

That girl has got a large round hat,
Perhaps a round red face;
We cannot judge how this may be,
But only of her grace.

JULY 9TH.

Currants black, and currants red,
Let's have some in a pie,
With sugar and delicious cream,—
We'll have some by-and-by.

JULY 10TH.

Letty and Etty walked hand in hand,
Pleasantly, quietly through the broad land;
Letty and Etty said, "Are we not good?
We walk and we talk just as little girls should."

JULY 11TH.

Lily, Lily, white and tall,
You are wondrous fair;
I bid you welcome to this book,
I'm glad you're standing there.

JULY 12TH.

Little Phillipina stands to watch the sun,
Thinks she'll stand and watch it till its work is done;
Little Phillipina, you must watch all day,
For the sun will shine till night, and then he'll go away.

JULY

JULY 13TH.

I look at this, and here is seen
A little sprig of creeping bean;
I like to eat them, I like them growing,
I like them in this picture showing.

JULY 14TH.

Do you like gooseberries? I can't say I do;
Perhaps you like currants, and raspberries too.
I wish you could come to our country home;
How much in the garden you would like to roam!

JULY 15TH.

To market they go, on St. Swithin's day,
They've something to sell, and something to pay;
They've one big umbrella to keep off the rain,
Which comes, on that Saint's day, again and again.

JULY 16TH.

It's very sad to stand alone,
    Upon a summer's day,
And long to see some chubby child,
    To have a game at play.

JULY 17TH.

A bramble once looked over a rail,
  "We shall have some rain," she said;
"Well, it's time that the grass should have a drink,
  And it's time that the dust was laid.'

JULY 18TH.

White and blue convolvulus!
    At four it goes to bed,
With bell closed tight with all its might,
    Perhaps you've heard it said?

JULY

JULY 19TH.

This funny old woman takes care of her dog,
  Her sun-shade protects her and it ;
"It's the dog-days, you know, and think, if poor Flo
  Went mad," said she, "and then bit !"

JULY 20TH.

The shuttlecock up in the air has flown,
  Oh, where, and oh, where is it gone ?
Alack and alack ! will it never come back ?
  The battledore's left all forlorn.

JULY 21ST.

This is Johnny, who says, " I've heard the hen cackle,
  I'm sure that some eggs she has laid ;
I'll go to the hen-house, and fill my basket—
  That is, if I don't feel afraid."

JULY 22ND.

When we have the warm, warm sunshine,
  That is when the flowers grow ;
In the garden, by the footpath,
  Stand the flowers in a row.

JULY 23RD.

Up the post the rose-tree twines,
  With its blossoms sweet and fair ;
To its neighbour lends a grace—
  To the post, so plain and bare.

JULY 24TH.

Hurrah, hurrah, for harvest-time !
  Hurrah for the grain our land yields !
Hurrah, hurrah, for the harvest-home,
  For the yellow sheaves in the fields !

JULY

JULY 25TH.

As I went out to take the air,
    I met two maidens small;
I greeted them politely,
    But they answered not at all.

JULY 26TH.

A maiden went a-gleaning,
    Upon a summer's day;
She gleaned and gleaned a goodly sheaf,
    Then went upon her way.

JULY 27TH.

Tilly Toddles knocked her head
    A very hard, hard blow;
She loudly cried, and sadly sighed
    "Oh dear! it hurts me so!"

JULY 28TH.

When I have no flowers, I love the leaves so green;
And the dainty leaf of a creeping plant is prettiest
    to be seen;
And if I can have flowers, with them I leaves
    entwine,
So round the clustering blossoms lie the leaves of
    the creeping vine.

JULY 29TH.

This girl has got the baby, I hope she will take care;
I think she might forget it—forget that it is there.
She wears so large a bonnet, that she really cannot see;
And she might drop the baby, and then how sad
    'twould be!

JULY 30TH.

"My greatest delight," said Timothy White,
    "Is to swing by my arms all day;
To me people call, 'Pray come down, you
    will fall;'
    But I laugh, and continue my play."

JULY * AUGUST

JULY 31ST.

Flowers yellow, leaves all green,
Here's a puffy ball between;
The children blow those balls away,
"They're clocks, and tell the time," they say.

AUGUST 1ST.

Here's a girl, she has a basket,
What is in it—do you ask it?
I heard a miow! it is a cat!
Now, children, what do you think of that?

AUGUST 2ND.

A small, small branch of a very large tree;
Pray, little folks, say what it may be?
It is shady and grand, and grows in our land,
And is reckoned a very fine tree.

AUGUST 3RD.

Tommy Thumbkin rides a barrel,—
Where does his journey lead?
To No-where Town, which is miles away,
He rides on his stalwart steed.

AUGUST 4TH.

A pot of flowers—oh, how sweet,
Flowers always are a treat;
In a garden or a pot,
We all love flowers—do we not?

AUGUST 5TH.

This tree grows in a garden,
Where merry children run;
They like this funny little tree,
It shelters them from sun.

AUGUST

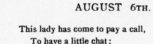

AUGUST 6TH.

This lady has come to pay a call,
    To have a little chat;
She talks of the weather, she talks of the news,
    She talks of this and of that.

AUGUST 7TH.

Poor croquet balls! quite idle,
    They've got no work to do;
Just like the frozen-out gardeners,
    That in winter trouble you.

AUGUST 8TH.

How doth the greedy little bee
    Take honey to his hive;
And sting, and buzz, and much annoy,
    And to be foremost strive.

AUGUST 9TH.

What does little Johnny see?—
    A waggon with horses four;
Each horse has a bell, and it jingles well,
    But Johnny wishes for more.

AUGUST 10TH.

Plums, plums, purple plums!
    Do you like them in a tart?
I like to pick them from the tree,
    And eat them, for my part.

AUGUST 11TH.

Flowers now are getting scarce,
    I regret to say;
How very, very sad 'twill be,
    When all are gone away!

AUGUST

AUGUST 12TH.

Upon a stile, beside a moor,
This boy sits quiet as a mouse;
He hears the sportsmen shooting near,
They're killing all the little grouse.

AUGUST 13TH.

What is this boy staring at?
    I dare say you wonder too;
Try as I may, I cannot say,
    But it must be something new.

AUGUST 14TH.

A player at croquet at last,
So it's not quite a thing of the past;
This girl is quite ready, with mallet in hand,
So I hope she won't have alone long to stand.

AUGUST 15TH.

This damsel seems extremely proud,
    Her nose so high in air;
I really don't think much of her,
    Such pride I cannot bear.

AUGUST 16TH.

What have you there, you dear little girl?
    What have you there, now tell?
Are they good, good things, you will have for tea;
    Or things that you want to sell?

AUGUST 17TH.

Out in the garden Miss Peachblossom ran,
A hat on her head, in her hand a great fan;
"I smell the sweet flowers—a bird past me flies;
Good-bye, pretty garden!" and back she then hies.

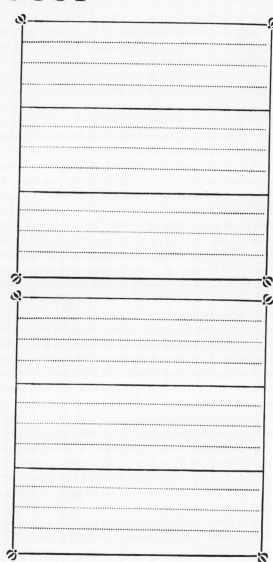

AUGUST

AUGUST 18TH.

Darling baby, as you look
Straight at me out of this book;
How I wish that I could take you,
And a real live baby make you?

AUGUST 19TH.

A very small man, with cocked hat so gay,
Remarkably active, he runs fast away;
A neat little figure, compact, and so brave,
As in triumph he lifts up his banner to wave.

AUGUST 20TH.

An Italian peasant, by a well;
Who she is I cannot tell;
She wears a very curious cap,
Awkward, if she took a nap.

AUGUST 21ST.

A storm in a tea-pot, I declare!
  Do tell me what's the matter!
This little person's quite put out,
  That's why there's such a clatter.

AUGUST 22ND.

A train goes by, and Tommy runs,
  And holds a flag quite high;
It is such fun, small Tommy thinks,
  To see a train go by.

AUGUST 23RD.

This girl is waiting for somebody,
  For whom is she waiting, I say?
I think it's for the pedlar,
  Who often comes this way.

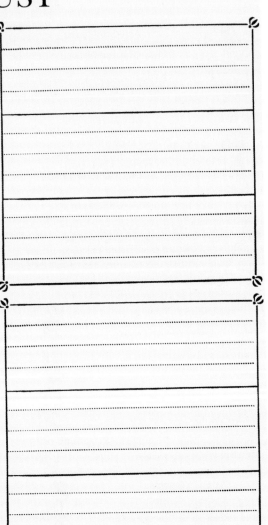

AUGUST

AUGUST 24TH.

Peter is running, oh, running!
And why does he run so fast?
He teased an old hen, who flew at him then,
And he thinks she will catch him at last.

AUGUST 25TH.

Eliza Jane she goes to market,
Upon a market day;
You'd like to know why it is so?
Well, really, I can't say.

AUGUST 26TH.

An old person once said, "I will try,
A very large bonnet to buy;
The neighbours will see,
And all envy me
This very large bonnet I buy "

AUGUST 27TH.

Little Hodge-Podge, he sat on a stile,
He thought that he would rest awhile;
He dozed, and dozed, and fell asleep,
And then fell in the ditch so deep.

AUGUST 28TH.

Now Dolly, dear Dolly, I'll put you to bed;
I have a big apron, a cap on my head;
You know I'm Nurse Crabbed, and very severe;
So take care you are good—now mind that,
Dolly dear.

AUGUST 29TH.

The two twin Master Twinklebys
Are good and quiet boys;
They neither tear their sister's hair,
Nor do they cry for toys.

231

AUGUST * SEPTEMBER

AUGUST 30TH.

What a big umbrella! and oh, what a hat!
What a curious person is he!
I've travelled for many and many a mile,
Yet the like of him never did see.

AUGUST 31ST.

Grapes, grapes! don't you like them
Purple, large and sweet!
Little children, come and pick them.
Come, and let us eat.

SEPTEMBER 1ST.

There was an old person who heard
Some shots fired near, at a bird;
Said he, "Now I remember,
'Tis the first of September;
But there flies the fortunate bird."

SEPTEMBER 2ND.

Here there stands a little form,
So very lightly clad,
I really fear she will be cold;
And it seems quite too bad.

SEPTEMBER 3RD.

He's watching a balloon,
That went up this afternoon;
It's gone so very high, right into the blue sky,
But it's sure to come down soon.

SEPTEMBER 4TH.

This is dejected Ann,
Look at her while you can;
She will not skip, and I'm really fearful
She'll melt away, she is so tearful.

SEPTEMBER

SEPTEMBER 5TH.

Baby ran to meet me, she had a sash all blue,
    A bran-new gown,
    Just come from town,
A cap so crisp and new.

SEPTEMBER 6TH.

A goodly melon,
    Colours green and yellow;
Flavour most delicious,
    Sweet and very mellow!

SEPTEMBER 7TH.

Going to school in the morning,
    With her bag by her side, and her slate;
She stands and stares at the passers-by,
    I'm sure that she will be late.

SEPTEMBER 8TH

Here I am, with mallet and ball—
    Who is going to play?
It is no use for me to stand
    And wait for you all day.

SEPTEMBER 9TH.

Apples, rosy-cheeked apples!
    Clustering on the tree;
I'd give you one, or give you two,
    If they belonged to me.

SEPTEMBER 10TH.

Thomasina looks afar,
    She sees a train go by;
"I declare that this minute I wish I was
      in it,"
    Thomasina said, with a sigh.

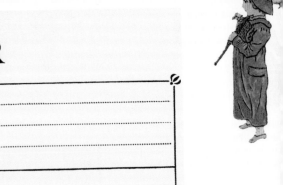

SEPTEMBER

SEPTEMBER 11TH.

Yes, see her standing there,
   Watering flowers;
She loves her garden,
   And works there for hours

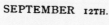

SEPTEMBER 12TH.

Lawn-tennis this girl thinks a very fine game;
Perhaps, little friends, you all think the same;
You have to be active, and you get very hot,
And the boys are the best at it—now, are they not?

SEPTEMBER 13TH.

Just a branch with apples,
   Tinted red and green;
The prettiest branch with apples
   That I have ever seen.

SEPTEMBER 14TH.

A girl sat on a wall one day,
She was tired, and would not play;
I called, "You'll fall," from the foot of the hill,
But she paid no heed, and sat there still.

SEPTEMBER 15TH.

There she stands at the garden gate,
But she has come so very late;
The flowers are going, the leaves now fall,
'Twere better, perhaps, if she came not at all.

SEPTEMBER 16TH.

A sweet, fair maiden rested on the plain;
Rested, and went, and never came again;
Oh! little maid, now dreary is the spot,
Oh! little maid, 'tis there, but you are not.

SEPTEMBER

SEPTEMBER 17TH.

Two brave stacks of famous hay,
Well stacked upon a summer day;
The birds think, as they homeward fly,
Some hay will keep our nests quite dry.

SEPTEMBER 18TH.

Oh, dear me, what a flurry!
You seem in a desperate hurry;
 You keep up such a pace,
 Are you running in a race,
That you fly along in a scurry?

SEPTEMBER 19TH.

Gaily dancing, tripping along,
Jumping high, and singing a song;
In your hair you've put a rose—
I think you rather want some clothes.

SEPTEMBER 20TH.

One large apple! is it for me?
Who has picked it off the tree?
We'll have it peeled, and put in a pie,
And then we'll eat it, you and I.

SEPTEMBER 21ST.

I should think it very hard,
 And also rather sad,
To dance alone, with so much grace—
 Indeed, it is too bad.

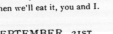

SEPTEMBER 22ND.

Polly has got a new Bow-wow,
 Polly is merry and gay;
Polly thinks the whole world bright,
 And this the happiest day.

236

SEPTEMBER

SEPTEMBER 23RD.

Digging, digging in the sands,
    With a bran-new spade;
Piling up the sand so high,
    Until a castle's made.

SEPTEMBER 24TH.

He's trying to catch a great big fish
And then he'll put it in a dish;
He and his wife on it will sup,
Perhaps they'll eat the monster up.

SEPTEMBER 25TH.

Reading a book with a steadfast look,
    So studiously inclined;
To run away with child and book,
    I think I've half a mind.

SEPTEMBER 26TH.

Johnny and Julia, two good little things,
    Sat on the ground together;
They talked of the birds, and talked of
    the trees.
    Enjoying the sunshiny weather.

SEPTEMBER 27TH.

A very big apple, a very large pear—
A nice dessert for us to share;
Let us divide them both in two,
And take two halves, both I and you.

SEPTEMBER 28TH.

Run, run, Elizabeth, run very fast!
If you don't catch it, the ball will go past;
Run, run, Elizabeth! see, it will fall!
Make haste, or else you won't catch it at all.

SEPTEMBER * OCTOBER

SEPTEMBER 29TH.

A large dish of grapes!
   Come, come, let us eat;
I think, for you little ones
   This is a treat.

SEPTEMBER 30TH.

Who has been in the woods to-day?
   Who has been there a-nutting?
With long-hooked sticks, and baskets too;
   The branches they've been cutting.

OCTOBER 1ST.

This is the day that the pheasants dread,
For the poor little things are shot through the
   head;
This little boy will help covers to beat,
And then there'll be plenty of pheasants to eat.

OCTOBER 2ND.

This boy is going to sail his boat,
   In a certain pond so round;
The pond is in Kensington Gardens—
   You know it, I'll be bound.

OCTOBER 3RD.

Oh, here we are in the country!
   Look at this bowl of cream!
And, you will see, five-o'clock tea
Delightful now will seem.

OCTOBER 4TH.

Out of the sweet, sweet flowers
   This funny goblin sprang;
And all the roses shook their heads,
   And all the blue-bells rang.

OCTOBER

OCTOBER 5TH.

A girl went walking by herself,
  The wind was rather high;
"Blow hard, old wind!" this bold girl cried,
  "I do not care, not I."

OCTOBER 6TH.

Phœbe has a new battledore
  And a new shuttlecock too:
"I shall send you flying, shuttlecock,",
  Said Phœbe, "that's what I ll do"

OCTOBER 7TH.

There has been rain, on the ground is dirt
  And so Cecilia holds up her skirt;
She holds her skirt, you see, quite high,
  To keep it clean, and also dry.

OCTOBER 8TH.

A Bishop's-thumb, I do declare!—
That is the name of this queer pear;
Were I a Bishop, I should fidget,
To have so oddly-shaped a digit.

OCTOBER 9TH.

"What are you looking at, Sally?" said she,
  "What do you see round there?"
"I see an old woman who rides a cock-horse,
  And a maiden with golden hair."

OCTOBER 10TH.

Come and play at cricket now,
  Come along, you boys;
Mind how you come, and quickly come,
  And do not make a noise.

OCTOBER

OCTOBER 11TH.

What fun children have,
　When the horse-chesnuts come !
They peel them, and string them—
　Now go and get some.

OCTOBER 12TH.

" Where are you going this morning ?
Where are you going this morning ?
" I hear the Queen is to be seen,
And I'm going to see her this morning.

OCTOBER 13TH.

Here's a pear—
Not here, but there ;
I mean, in the book,
If you will but look.

OCTOBER 14TH.

What is this boy fishing for ?
　What does he hope to get ?
He hopes to get a very fine fish,
　But I think he will get wet.

OCTOBER 15TH.

Why does she cry, this dear little trot ?
　And why does she suck her thumb ?
It cannot be sweet—it is horrid to eat ;
　So, instead, let us give her a plum.

OCTOBER 16TH.

Tabitha has a hoop to bowl,
　And Tabitha's very glad ;
Tabitha had no hoop one day,
　Then Tabitha was sad.

OCTOBER

OCTOBER 17TH.

This boy now sees a large, large ship,
   That's sailing out to sea ;
His heart is sore, for one he loves
   Must in that large ship be.

OCTOBER 18TH.

John and Joan go up to town,
   London town to view ;
"The streets are gold, so we are told ;
   We'll see, both I and you."

OCTOBER 19TH.

"I've a nice new bonnet," an old dame said,
   "It shelters me well, I know ;
Some people think it a trifle large,
   And perhaps it may be so."

OCTOBER 20TH.

Janet didn't know her lesson,
   Janet said it badly ;
Janet was rebuked severely,
   Janet took it sadly.

OCTOBER 21ST.

"Hip, hip, hurrah!" cried Jonathan Green,
   "The Queen will soon pass by ;
I don't care a mite for all the grand sight,
   But to see the Queen I'll try."

OCTOBER 22ND.

"Ride, little brother, ride on my back ;
   Where shall we go to now ?
Up to the sty, to see the pig,
   To the meadow to see the cow ?"

OCTOBER

OCTOBER 23RD.

Sammy has a little line,
    H s mother has a dish,
On which small Sammy trusts that he
    May shortly place a fish.

OCTOBER 24TH.

Little fairy in a shell, sailing o'er the sea!
Whither are you coming?—perhaps to visit me.
Where, then, do you come from, o'er the stormy
        main?
Little fairy, how I trust you'll get back safe again!

OCTOBER 25TH.

Little Polly has an old dolly,
    She loves it—oh, so dearly!
She cannot see how ugly it be,
    Though we can, very clearly.

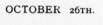

OCTOBER 26TH.

Sweet little girl, now where do you look?
    Do tell me what it can be.
"I'm looking and longing for my Mamma,
    And she is across the sea."

OCTOBER 27TH.

Turnips, if done in this way,
Will cure a cold, so they say:
Cut the turnips into slices, put them in a pan,
A little water, some brown sugar, and—eat
        them if you can.

OCTOBER 28TH.

Now listen, while I tell you
    About this little maid,
Who went out with her Mamma—
    But now it all is said.

OCTOBER * NOVEMBER

OCTOBER 29TH.

Little Baby's dressed, and waits—
    Dressed to go a-tata ;
Who do you think he's going with ?
    He's going out with Papa.

OCTOBER 30TH.

The leaves are turning brown and dry.
They fall all round as we pass by ;
The country looks all cold and drear,
No flowers, no fruit, no birds are here.

OCTOBER 31ST.

Here's a jar of apples,
    And here we have a pan ;
'Tis Allhallow E'en,
And now, I ween,
    You've all the fun you can.

NOVEMBER 1ST.

This is little Hodge we see,
Sitting down and having tea ;
Let us hope the tea is hot,
For sure it is, the weather's not.

NOVEMBER 2ND.

Penelope goes to see her aunt,
    And sits demure and prim ;
For Auntie is an ancient maid,
    Both angular and slim.

NOVEMBER 3RD.

Here is a pair of pears !
    Cissy and you are a pair ;
Let us divide the pair of pears
    Between the other pair.

NOVEMBER

NOVEMBER 4TH.

Darling little Lily has this Birthday Book,
Into it the little child casts many and many a look;
And I know she likes it—so, I hope, do you;
It's made to please the children—that I always try to do.

NOVEMBER 5TH.

Remember, my friends, 'tis the fifth of November;
    This is a fine guy, is he not?
When such creatures we see, no reason there'll be,
    Why Guy Fawkes' Day should e'er be forgot.

NOVEMBER 6TH.

I stand upon the shore
And hear the great waves roar;
I see the great ships tost,
And pray that none be lost.

NOVEMBER 7TH.

What can I give you, Ma'am, to-day?
    Sausage, ham, or mutton-pie,
Beef, or tongue, or chickens fine?
    To please your taste, Ma'am, I will try.

NOVEMBER 8TH

Leafless trees are standing bare,
    Against the cold autumnal sky;
Alas, for the buds and blossoms gone
    Alas, for the summer past! we sigh.

NOVEMBER 9TH.

What is Harry looking at,
    Why does he stand and stare?
He sees a grand sight, that gives him delight,
    The Lord Mayor's Procession is there!

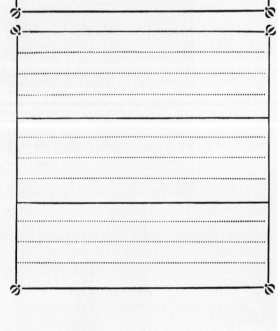

NOVEMBER

NOVEMBER 10TH.

You see, little Anna has got a large dish
    Of apples so rosy and fair;
She is coming this way, so I very much hope
    She'll invite all her friends here to share.

NOVEMBER 11TH.

Here's a little milkmaid,
    Very welcome, too;
Give us some nice milk to drink,
    Little milkmaid, do!

NOVEMBER 12TH.

This girl has just come back from school,
    She sits and rests awhile;
She's rather tired now, you know,
    For she's walked many a mile.

NOVEMBER 13TH.

"I must go to the stables,
    I must hie to the barn;
I must look to the horses,
    And see they come to no harm."

NOVEMBER 14TH.

"Oh, buy my oranges! buy, I pray!
    I'm very—very poor;
You're warm and happy in your homes,
    I stand cold at the door."

NOVEMBER 15TH.

A very old goblin lives in this tower,
    He eats nothing but mustard and batter;
And why should he choose such very odd fare?
    I will tell you—he's mad as a hatter.

NOVEMBER

NOVEMBER 16TH.

She walked along, with her bonnet so big,
And she carried her bag by her side,
"Ho, ho! there's a fine old girl, to be sure!"
The rude street-boys then cried.

NOVEMBER 17TH.

Polly Perkins carries a pan,
What is in it? guess, if you can;
Perhaps it's some water to wash her face,
But I can't say she carries the pan with much grace.

NOVEMBER 18TH.

This is Miss Jessie, she looks rather prim,
With her nice great-coat and her hat so trim;
Where is she going, this cold day?
I do not know, so cannot say.

NOVEMBER 19TH.

How cold she must be, that poor little mite!
Look at her little bare arm;
I hope that Jack Frost won't give her a bite,
That the weather will not do her harm.

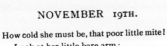

NOVEMBER 20TH.

Strike the tree, woodman,
Strike, strike away!
Strike, strike the grand old tree,
Strike while you may!

NOVEMBER 21ST.

A lady went a-walking,
She was so fair, so fair!
Alas! it is a picture,
She is not really there.

NOVEMBER

NOVEMBER 22ND.

Jack was such a clever boy!
" I like to work," he said;
You see, he now goes off to school,
To cram his busy head.

NOVEMBER 23RD.

What do you think of her?
I think she's plain;
If you ask me once more,
I shall say so again.

NOVEMBER 24TH.

Here's a little woman,
Carrying a large tray
Where does she come from?
Guess it now you may.

NOVEMBER 25TH.

Little folks, here's an empty chair,
See how many of you it can bear;
Do you think two, do you think three?
I think that depends on how heavy you be.

NOVEMBER 26TH.

A very long dress, and a queer frilled cap,
She carries a basket, too;
I've no more to say,
Perhaps, though, you may:
I am not so clever as you.

NOVEMBER 27TH.

A brigand's hat! well, what of that,
If there's no head within?
To take off one without the other,
I really call a sin.

NOVEMBER * DECEMBER

NOVEMBER 28TH.

This is Obadiah,
Who walks on the sands,
And carries a pail
In his little hands.

NOVEMBER 29TH.

Have pity, children, on the poor
Their days are full of woe;
They have few clothes, so little food,
No home where they can go.

NOVEMBER 30TH.

There was an old man who was bent,
And over his stick he oft leant;
He said, "But for my sticks,
I should be in a fix,
For I really am terribly bent."

DECEMBER 1ST.

This is a screen, a hand-screen,
A screen that came from China!
And who do you think, now, gave it me?
Why it was cousin Dinah.

DECEMBER 2ND.

A tiny house, a nice wee house,
A house that just suits me;
And when we're really settled there,
I hope you'll come and see.

DECEMBER 3RD.

Sweep, sweep, old woman,
Sweep, sweep away;
Sweep all the dust and dirt,
Fast as you may.

DECEMBER

DECEMBER 4TH.

This is Phil, who says he's ill,
And cannot go to school;
He's running just the other way
He will grow up a fool

DECEMBER 5TH.

On a cold, cold day in December,
Delightful it is, to be sure,
To sit in front of the fire;
But take care there's no draught
from the door.

DECEMBER 6TH.

This is Angelina, going for a walk,
She can smile so pleasantly, and so nicely talk;
She is indeed so sweet a child, that like her there are few
She is a dear good little girl, and so, perhaps, are you.

DECEMBER 7TH.

Here's a handsome cup, I wonder what is in it?
Give a guess now, children, say what you think,
this minute;
Lily says it's chocolate, Johnny says it's tea;
Now, children, what do you say? Please to tell
it me.

DECEMBER 8TH.

Certainly she's tall and slight,
Certainly a weight quite light;
Certainly I don't admire
This tall, straight dame, or her attire.

DECEMBER 9TH.

Poor little beggar-girl, out in the cold!
Show pity, all you who have silver and gold;
Give from your plenty all you can spare,
With the poor and the wretched be willing to share.

DECEMBER

DECEMBER 10TH.

A broom in his hand, a mop on his head,
    A little merry boy;
Few playthings he has, so he takes the broom,
    To serve him for a toy.

DECEMBER 11TH.

This is good Mr. Longnose,
    For his learning famed, and sense;
P'rhaps the knowledge he has gained
    Has made his nose immense.

DECEMBER 12TH.

See, what a poor little ragged lad!
It really makes me very sad
To see a boy in such a state;
Now think, how very hard his fate.

DECEMBER 13TH.

Phœbe sits upon a stool,
    Of legs it has but three;
It may be big enough for her,
    But not for you or me.

DECEMBER 14TH.

Here we are on a cold, cold night,
Rolled up warm, so nice and tight;
Going off to see a play,
At the close of a winter's day.

DECEMBER 15TH.

What do you want now, Billy?
What do you want, I say?
    "I've been a good boy,
    So I want a toy,
And a plum-bun this day."

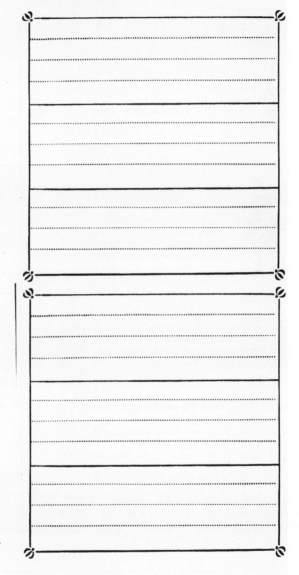

DECEMBER

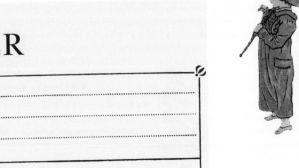

DECEMBER 16TH.

Here's a merry lad, I ween,
Happy he, as King or Queen;
Glad is he to take your penny,
Still he smiles if you've not any.

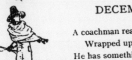

DECEMBER 17TH.

A coachman ready for the road,
  Wrapped up from chin to toes;
He has something tragic on his mind,
  Which troubles ere he goes.

DECEMBER 18TH.

I think we come upon a fancy ball,
Or else I cannot make him out at all;
His curious hat, with large and drooping feather,
His dress, unsuited to the time or weather

DECEMBER 19TH.

A Dresden china figure this,
  How pretty, children—look!
We really find some curious things
  Within this Birthday Book.

DECEMBER 20TH.

And where do you come from, with shillalagh in your
    hand?
"Shure, and plase yer honor, I come from Paddyland,
Auld Ireland, the island of praties and milk;
And shure, blarney, too—ain't our tongues soft as silk?"

DECEMBER 21ST.

What archer is this? Why, bold Robin Hood;
He has left all his men, and come out of the wood;
He thought you would like to handle the bow,
So the best way to do so he thought he would show.

DECEMBER

DECEMBER 22ND.

This is Hang-me-up-hi, the mandarin,
As grand a Chinese as ever was seen;
Look at his pigtail, look at his toes,
And all his very magnificent clothes.

DECEMBER 23RD.

Here's another little fellow,
  In fancy dress you see;
A little cavalier, I think
  That he must really be.

DECEMBER 24TH.

Christmas Eve! Now, all you merry children,
  Hang up your stockings, and sink to happy rest;
Then gliding through the room the Christ-child passes,
  And breathing near the sleepers, leaves them blest.

DECEMBER 25TH.

Christmas! Hear the joy-bells ringing,
Glad hymns in the churches singing;
Of His mercy, of His power,
And the gifts good angels shower!

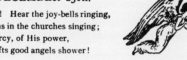

DECEMBER 26TH.

Why does she wear a steeple stuck upon her head?
This is a mediæval dress, so I've heard it said;
Why has she got a battledore and shuttlecock in
    hand?
To tell the truth, this lady I cannot understand.

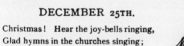

DECEMBER 27TH.

A person once said "I will run;
You can have no idea of the fun
    Of running so fast
    That you drop down at last,
And feel that you're utterly done."

DECEMBER

DECEMBER 28TH.

Little Bo-peep, I declare,
  With little hat and crook!
How nice to find so old a friend
  Within the Birthday Book.

DECEMBER 29TH.

Yes, I was sure of it, sure as could be,
And yet he would not listen to me;
He kicked his legs, and he made them sore,
With those ridiculous spurs he wore!

DECEMBER 30TH.

This looks to me like a dreadful robber;
  Is it he who left the "Babes in the Wood"
To perish sadly with cold and hunger,
  Covered with leaves by the dickies good?

DECEMBER 31ST.

This old woman takes a fly,
To sweep the cobwebs off the sky.
She says, "As I'm going up so high,
I wish the Old Year, and you all, Good-bye."

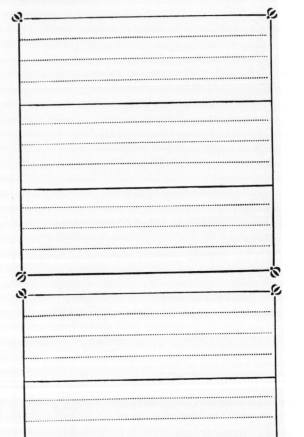

WHERE ARE YOU GOING TO, MY PRETTY MAID?

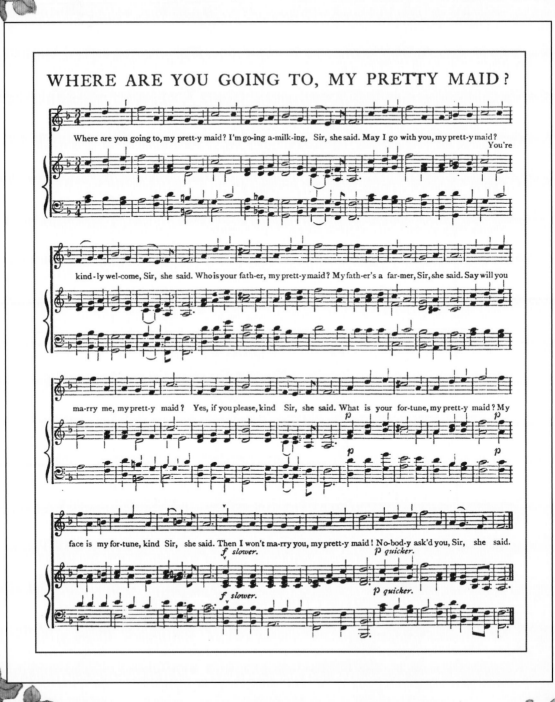

Where are you going to, my prett-y maid? I'm go-ing a-milk-ing, Sir, she said. May I go with you, my prett-y maid? You're

kind-ly wel-come, Sir, she said. Who is your fath-er, my prett-y maid? My fath-er's a far-mer, Sir, she said. Say will you

ma-rry me, my prett-y maid? Yes, if you please, kind Sir, she said. What is your for-tune, my prett-y maid? My

face is my for-tune, kind Sir, she said. Then I won't ma-rry you, my prett-y maid! No-bod-y ask'd you, Sir, she said.

Book of Tunes

Selections from the original,
illustrated by Kate Greenaway

CURLY LOCKS.

Curly Locks, Curly Locks, wilt thou be mine ?
Thou shalt not wash dishes nor yet feed the swine,
But sit on a cushion and sew a fine seam,
And feed upon strawberries, sugar, and cream.

HUSH-A-BYE, BABY.

Hush-a-bye, baby, on the tree top,
When the wind blows the cradle will rock;
When the bough breaks the cradle will fall,
And down comes baby and cradle and all.

JACK AND JILL.

Jack and Jill went up the hill
To fetch a pail of water;
Jack fell down and broke his crown,
And Jill came tumbling after.

SING A SONG OF SIXPENCE.

LITTLE MISS MUFFET.

Little Miss Muffet
Sat on a tuffet,
Eating her curds and whey;
When down came a spider,
And sat down beside her,
And frighten'd Miss Muffet away.

MARY, MARY, QUITE CONTRARY.

Mary, Mary, quite contrary,
How does your garden grow ?
With silver bells and cockle shells,
And pretty maids all of a row.

LITTLE POLLY FLINDERS.

Little Polly Flinders
Sat on the cinders,
Warming her little toes;
Her mother came and caught her,
And scolded her little daughter,
For spoiling her nice new clothes.

PUSSY CAT, PUSSY CAT.

Pussy Cat, Pussy Cat, where have you been ?
I've been to London to look at the Queen.
Pussy Cat, Pussy Cat, what did you there ?
I frighten'd a little mouse under the chair.

SING A SONG OF SIXPENCE.

Sing a song of sixpence, a pocket full of rye,
Four-and-twenty blackbirds baked in a pie;
When the pie was open'd the birds began to sing,
Was not that a dainty dish to set before a King.

WHERE ARE YOU GOING TO, MY PRETTY MAID ?

Where are you going to, my pretty maid ?
I'm going a-milking, Sir, she said.
May I go with you, my pretty maid ?
You're kindly welcome, Sir, she said.
Who is your father, my pretty maid ?
My father's a farmer, Sir, she said.
Say will you marry me, my pretty maid ?
Yes, if you please, kind Sir, she said.
What is your fortune, my pretty maid ?
My face is my fortune, kind Sir, she said.
Then I won't marry you, my pretty maid
Nobody ask'd you, Sir, she said.

GENTLE JESUS, MEEK AND MILD.

Gentle Jesus, meek and mild,
Look upon a little child;
Pity my simplicity,
Suffer me to come to Thee,
Gentle Jesus, meek and mild.

Fain I would to Thee be brought,
Dearest Lord, forbid it not;
In the kingdom of Thy grace
Grant a little child a place,
Gentle Jesus, meek and mild.

GENTLE JESUS, MEEK AND MILD.

Gen - tle Je - sus, meek and mild, Look u - pon a lit - tle child; Pit - y my sim -
Fain I would to Thee be brought, Dear-est Lord, for - bid it not; In the king - dom

plic - i - ty, Suf - fer me to come to Thee, Gen - tle Jes - us, meek and mild.
of Thy grace Grant a lit - tle child a place.